Stratification and Inequality Series
The Center for the Study of Social Stratification and Inequality,
Global COE Program
Tohoku University, Japan
Volume 11

Minorities and Diversity

Stratification and Inequality Series

The Center for the Study of Social Stratification and Inequality,
Global COE Program
Tohoku University, Japan

Inequality amid Affluence: Social Stratification in Japan
Junsuke Hara and Kazuo Seiyama

Intentional Social Change: A Rational Choice Theory
Yoshimichi Sato

Constructing Civil Society in Japan: Voices of Environmental Movements
Koichi Hasegawa

Deciphering Stratification and Inequality: Japan and beyond
Yoshimichi Sato

Social Justice in Japan: Concepts, Theories and Paradigms
Ken-ichi Ohbuchi

Gender and Career in Japan
Atsuko Suzuki

Status and Stratification:
Cultural Forms in East and Southeast Asia
Mitsuhiko Shima

Globalization, Minorities and Civil Society:
Perspectives from Asian and Western Cities
Koichi Hasegawa and Naoki Yoshihara

Fluidity of Place: Globalization and the Transformation of Urban Space
Naoki Yoshihara

Japan's New Inequality: Intersection of
Employment Reforms and Welfare Arrangements
Yoshimichi Sato and Jun Imai

Minorities and Diversity
Kunihiro Kimura

Series Editor: Yoshimichi Sato, Tohoku University

Editorial Board: Koichi Hasegawa, Ken-ichi Ohbuchi, Toshiaki Kimura, Kunihiro Kimura, Yoshimichi Sato, Naoki Yoshihara, Mary C. Brinton, Jeffrey P. Broadbent

Stratification and Inequality Series
The Center for the Study of Social Stratification and Inequality,
Global COE Program
Tohoku University, Japan
Volume 11

Minorities and Diversity

Edited by

Kunihiro Kimura

This English edition first published in 2011 by
Trans Pacific Press, PO Box 164, Balwyn North, Melbourne, Victoria 3104, Australia
Telephone: +61-3-9859-1112 Fax: +61-3-9859-4110
Email: tpp.mail@gmail.com
Web: http://www.transpacificpress.com

Copyright © Trans Pacific Press 2011

Copy-edited by Miriam Riley

Designed and set by digital environs, Melbourne. http://www.digitalenvirons.com

Printed by BPA Print Group, Burwood, Victoria, Australia

Distributors

Australia and New Zealand
DA Information Services/Central Book Services
648 Whitehorse Road
Mitcham, Victoria 3132
Australia
Telephone: +61-3-9210-7777
Fax: + 61-3-9210-7788
Email: books@dadirect.com
Web: www.dadirect.com

USA and Canada
International Specialized Book Services (ISBS)
920 NE 58th Avenue, Suite 300
Portland, Oregon 97213-3786
USA
Telephone: 1-800-944-6190
Fax: 1-503-280-8832
Email: orders@isbs.com
Web: http://www.isbs.com

Asia and the Pacific
Kinokuniya Company Ltd.

Head office:
3-7-10 Shimomeguro
Meguro-ku
Tokyo 153-8504
Japan
Telephone: +81-3-6910-0531
Fax: +81-3-6420-1362
Email: bkimp@kinokuniya.co.jp
Web: www.kinokuniya.co.jp

Asia-Pacific office:
Kinokuniya Book Stores of Singapore Pte., Ltd.
391B Orchard Road #13-06/07/08
Ngee Ann City Tower B
Singapore 238874
Telephone: +65-6276-5558
Fax: +65-6276-5570
Email: SSO@kinokuniya.co.jp

All rights reserved. No production of any part of this book may take place without the written permission of Trans Pacific Press.

ISBN 978-1-920901-64-6 (Hardback)
ISBN 978-1-920901-88-2 (Paperback)

Image copyright: toronto.reaction, 2011, used under licence from shutterstock.com.

Contents

Figures vi
Tables vii
Preface ix

1 Gender-Based Discrimination, Inequality, and Marriage
  Kunihiro Kimura 1
2 Single Mothers and Child Support Policies in Japan
  Miyuki Shimoebisu 15
3 Women's Roles and Gender Order in Early Modern and
  Modern Japan *Rumi Matsuzaki* 31
4 Diversifying Korean Populations in Japan and a New
  Type of Ethnic Movement *Hyun Sun Lee* 51
5 Dealing with the Past: The Construction of Subjectivity
  in the Japanese American Reparation Movement
  Kumiko Tsuchida 67
6 Reflexive Modernity and Young Muslims: Identity
  Management in a Diverse Area in the UK *Satoshi Adachi* 83
7 Status, Selection, and Exchange in an Okinawan Mutual
  Aid System *Masahiro Tsujimoto* 100
8 Cultivating Social Diversity and the Role of NGOs/NPOs
  Kōichi Hasegawa 113

Notes 136
Bibliography 142
Index 154

Figures

1.1	Percentage of unmarried women in Japan, 1965–2005	2
1.2	The decision-making tree for a woman	3
1.3	Gender wage gap (M_f/M_m) for two age groups in Japan, 1965–2005	7
1.4	Difference in the proportion of regular employees for unmarried and married women	8
1.5	Standard deviation of income for regular employees by gender and age group	9
3.1	The structure of the channels through *omote* and *oku*	37
3.2	The relation by marriage between the Shimazu family and the Konoe family	38
3.3	The structure of the Shimazu family in early modern times	48
3.4	The structure of the Shimazu family in the Meiji period	49
3.5	The structure of the Shimazu family in the Taishō period	49
8.1	Japan's IMD international competitiveness ranking	115
8.2	The proportion of women in leadership positions in various fields	123
8.3	Number of specified nonprofit organizations (December 1998 to October 2010)	125
8.4	Knowledge of NPOs	126

Tables

1.1	Percentages of unmarried women: estimated and actual values	11
2.1	Divorced single mothers and child support	16
2.2	Single parents receiving child support	20
2.3	Two child support policy models	26
6.1	Social attributes of informants	89
7.1	ROSCAs as of July, 2005	105
7.2	Result of follow-up study	107
8.1	Top 30 in the IMD international competitiveness scale (2010)	116
8.2	Categories of activities of incorporated NPOs	127

Preface

The study of minorities has accrued findings and posed theories on segregation and prejudice in conjunction with the study of social stratification and inequality. However, the existence of minorities in society does not necessarily lead to effects that are considered socially 'negative' by specialists in the field. Rather, in recent times new theories and concepts that propose 'positive' meanings are emerging, while maintaining focus on the mechanisms that produce segregation, prejudice, and inequality.

The crucial concept that embodies this change in direction of minority studies is 'diversity.' This concept does not simply signify a description of diversified populations in society. Conversely, it represents an ideal that emphasizes the possibility that societal diversity realized through the existence of minorities results in a more creative society. It is true that minorities are segregated and suffer prejudice and inequality. Thus, in attempts to redress these forms of oppression and subjugation, we should proffer policies that connect the existence of minorities to the enrichment of society. This is the ideal behind the concept of 'diversity.' In western societies such as the US, diversity in this sense centers on ethnicity. However, if this is framed in the social context of Japan, the concept implies social change caused by the diversification of lifestyle and the emergence of various forms of family.

The title of this volume, *Minorities and Diversity*, embodies these theoretical tenets—empirically analyzing mechanisms that produce segregation, prejudice, and inequality surrounding minorities as well as normatively exploring the social conditions under which the existence of minority groups and social diversity are linked to creativity and dynamism. This volume represents the vibrant activities of the Division of the Study of Minorities (hereafter: the Division) at the Center for the Study of Social Stratification and Inequality at Tohoku University. The fundamental purpose of the Division is to explore the relationship between minority status and inequality. More concretely, members of the Division study the following topics to name a few: the status of women in the labor market, marriage and women, single motherhood, women in the early modern era, ethnic minorities, and ethnic identity. Chapters in this volume were created dialogically through the exchange of ideas at the Division.

The first three chapters examine the status of women in Japan from various perspectives. In Chapter One, I propose a decision-making model of marriage to explain the increase in the proportion of unmarried women in Japan. Although this is a model at the individual (micro) level, I pose two assumptions at the social (macro) level linking the distribution of income and marriage in order to create a micro–macro link. I then derive predictions from the model and test their empirical validity using official data. Although only one prediction is supported by the data, this simple model is a good point of departure for the development of better models explaining the increase in the proportion of unmarried women in Japan.

In Chapter Two, Miyuki Shimoebisu discusses the situation of single mothers in Japan comparing Japan's child support policy with that in Sweden, Germany, France, the US, and the UK. She focuses on the issue of paternal non-payment of child support following divorce. She points to the low level of compliance regarding child support payments from fathers in Japan, worsening the financial situation of single mothers. However, Japanese fathers are not necessarily exceptional. Non-payment is observed in the five societies discussed, necessitating the development of child support policies to resolve this problem in each case. After exploring the policies in the five societies, Shimoebisu argues that the main concern with the child support policy in Japan is that it fails as a family policy. Because family policy in Japan applies only to two-parent families, fathers and their children after divorce as well as single mothers fall outside of its scope. Thus, Shimoebisu proposes that Japan is in need of policy that ensures government child support to mitigate the hardships faced particularly by single mothers.

In Chapter Three, Rumi Matsuzaki explores changes in women's roles and gender order in Japan from the early modern to modern periods, focusing on the concepts of *omote* (the public sphere) and *oku* (the private sphere). She studies the Shimazu family, the feudal lord of the Satsuma domain, and commoners in order to paint a holistic picture of the changes. In the case of the Shimazu family, the legitimate wife and female vassals performed political functions through the *oku* channel to support the feudal lord. Although there was strict gender segregation between *omote* and *oku*, females in *oku* were not detached from social, economic, and political activities. However, modernization in Japan changed the structure of the Shimazu family resulting in the separation of enterprise and residence. Women in the Shimazu family then began to perform only domestic functions and were deprived of the political activities they were once committed to. Here we can observe the establishment of modern gender segregation during the modernization of Japan. In the case of commoners, the spatial differentiation between *omote* and *oku* did not exist, and the gendered division of labor was not as strict as that established in the Shimazu family. Matsuzaki's findings tell us that the gender divisions currently observable do not necessarily have solid foundations or a long history.

Chapters Four, Five, Six, and Seven study how minority groups solve their problems in relation to the majority, collectively and individually. In Chapter Four, Hyun Sun Lee analyzes changes in a Korean community (Chongryun) in Japan. This community has held a tight relationship with North Korea and supported Koreans in Japan through measures such as the provision of education through the Chongryun Korean school system. However, social antagonism against the community has grown in Japan due to North Korean militaristic activities, including the development of nuclear power in 1994, the missile experiment in 1998, and the abduction of Japanese citizens. To cope with this crisis, a new type of ethnic movement has been emerging in the community. Lee focuses on Aera, an organized movement of the new type. In contrast to the Chongryun community's stance against assimilation into Japanese society, Aera is actively involved in it and even obtained the status of a Nonprofit Organization (NPO) in order to provide Koreans, and in particular elderly Koreans, with social welfare services. Here Lee points to the increasing diversity of the Chongryun community and the new directions taken in efforts to address issues faced by Koreans in contemporary Japan.

In Chapter Five, Kumiko Tsuchida raises an interesting research question: why did Japanese Americans who had not experienced internment during the Second World War participate in a movement to claim reparation for it? Throughout this period Japanese Americans were forced to live in internment camps and the US government confiscated their property. It is thus understandable that those who experienced the internment sought reparation. However, it is more difficult to account for the participation of younger generation Japanese Americans in the reparation movement. To address the above conundrum, Tsuchida traces the life history of Mary Kimoto, a Japanese American who was an active member of the movement. Tsuchida reveals that Kimoto's participation in the movement facilitated her own search for identity. Before participating in the movement, she did not have a solid identity as a Japanese American. Legally she was American, but neither a 'white' American, the dominant group in the US, nor a Japanese. However, she overcame this identity crisis by indirectly experiencing the internment of older Japanese Americans to claim reparation. Thus Tsuchida answers her research question by pointing to the relationship between the identity of younger Japanese Americans and their participation in the reparation movement.

In Chapter Six, Satoshi Adachi explores how young Muslims in the UK strive to manage their identities. Young Muslims have had difficulties maintaining their identities in the UK especially since the 9/11 attacks of 2001 and the terrorist attacks in London in 2005. Following these events, the British government suddenly realized that common democratic values and identity, expressed in the concept of 'Britishness,' were needed to accommodate Muslims, especially the young, into mainstream society. However, such thinking is based on a biased assumption that young Muslims are segregated from the larger society and affected by radical Islamic teachings. Adachi challenges this assumption through the analysis of his interview data with young Muslims in Coventry, asking about their lives in and opinions of British society. His findings are positive. These youths befriend those of different ethnicity; distinguish between Islamic teachings and their ethnic values, facilitating smooth adaptation to British society; and even display tolerance towards those espousing anti-Muslim sentiments. These findings indicate that young Muslims are well equipped with democratic values as British citizens while enjoying and celebrating their Muslim identity and heritage. In other words, as an individual solution to their problems in the UK, these young people have negotiated the art of identity management and developed multi-faceted identities to adapt to British society. This process of identity management is similar to that described by Mary Kimoto in Chapter Five.

In Chapter Seven, Masahiro Tsujimoto examines a collective solution employed by Okinawan women to alleviate their hardships. They form rotating savings and credit associations (ROSCAs) to start businesses and cover emergent medical expenses. A ROSCA consists of a number of members, each of who contributes funds at its meetings. A member is then selected by rotation or a bidding system and receives the dues (the sum of the contributions). Thus ROSCAs are a kind of micro credit system and have substantively supported the lives of women in Okinawa. However, ROSCAs are always at the risk of defaulting. Members may not contribute money before or after they receive funds. As a result, promoters of ROSCAs have developed techniques to prevent default. Tsujimoto conducted a series of intensive interviews with a promoter to understand the techniques and dynamics of the ROSCAs she ran. The implications of this study extend beyond ROSCAs in Okinawa to address such topics as the provision of public goods and the prevention of free riders.

In the final chapter, Koichi Hasegawa proposes that Nongovernmental Organizations (NGOs) and NPOs can be viewed as a trigger for the increase in social diversity in Japan. He argues that contemporary Japan is in a deadlock: cultural diversity in Japan was possibly greater in the early modern period than today; Japan's international competitiveness has become weaker; the rise in the number of hereditary politicians has led to weak political leadership; and young Japanese are risk-averse, shunning opportunities to go abroad for better education and employment. To break this deadlock, Hasegawa proposes that an increase in social diversity would lead to a more vibrant and dynamic Japanese society. Increased participation of women in the public sphere and a larger intake of migrants are posed as positive solutions to this contention that have not yet been fully realized. Thus Hasegawa looks to NGOs and NPOs due to the advantages they have over companies and governments—national and local—in terms of their ability to enhance social diversity. Of course, there are obstacles to their activities. Hasegawa concludes this chapter by pointing to the importance and necessity of intermediaries that liaise between NGOs/NPOs and society and create networks of these organizations.

This volume would not have been published but for a grant offered by the Center for the Study of Social Stratification and Inequality at Tohoku University. I gratefully appreciate the Center's academic and financial support in this regard. I also thank Airin Izumi, Hiroaki Ozaki, Fukuo Ootomo, and Miho Kimura for their incredibly proficient secretarial work at the Center. Last but not least, I am profoundly grateful to Professor Yoshio Sugimoto of Trans Pacific Press for his marvelous editorial support.

Kunihiro Kimura
November 2010

1 Gender-Based Discrimination, Inequality, and Marriage

Kunihiro Kimura

Unmarried women in Japan: a growing sector

One of the characteristics of contemporary Japanese society is the increasing proportion of unmarried women. Figure 1.1 shows the trend for two key age groups, that is, 25–29 and 30–34.[1] From this figure we can see the rising diversity among women in terms of marital decision-making in particular and life course in general.

As economic analyses of marriage and family in terms of women's rational decision-making processes (e.g. Becker 1991; Santos 1975) have already suggested, the proportion of unmarried women may be increasing due to women's expanding economic independence. However, previous research contains three major problems. First, the research tends to straightforwardly and intuitively infer implications in terms of the societal outcomes (i.e. the macro-level conclusions) from a particular gendered model of agency (i.e. the micro-level assumptions). Second, the concept of economic independence is ambiguous; and third, only a few of the previous studies have tested their predictions using data analysis.

Thus, I proposed a simple model of marriage, which is an expected value model combined with assumptions on the distribution of income and the partnering of men and women, in order to explain the relationship between women's expanding economic independence and the proportion of unmarried women (Kimura 2000). This model not only established a micro–macro link but also provided us with falsifiable predictions on the effects of gender-based discrimination and income inequality within the institution of marriage.[2]

Nevertheless, thus far I have not tested these predictions. Thus, in this chapter, I want to address this gap and further test the estimated proportion of unmarried women from my model, using two survey data sets collected in Japan from 1965 to 2005.

I now briefly describe the model of marriage I proposed in 2000 (Kimura 2000), the predictions from the model, and the formula for

Figure 1.1: Percentage of unmarried women in Japan, 1965–2005

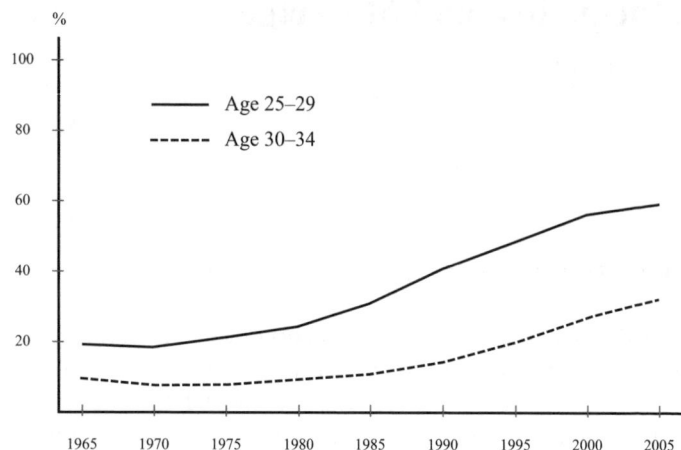

Source: National Census (Statistical Bureau, Management and Coordination Agency, Japan, 1967, 1972, 1977, 1982, 1987, 1991, 1996; Statistical Bureau, Ministry of Public Management, Home Affairs, Posts and Telecommunications, Japan 2001; Statistical Bureau, Ministry of Affairs and Communications, Japan 2006).

the estimation of the proportion of unmarried women I developed. Following this, I provide information on the data that I use in order to test these predictions and outline the estimation. I then present the results of the tests of these predictions and the estimation itself. Finally, I discuss the reasons behind the negative result and the implications of this study from the perspective of the diversification of women's life courses.

A simple model of marriage

Let me briefly describe my model of marriage (Kimura 2000). This model is basically an expected value model of a woman's decision-making process regarding marriage. Figure 1.2 shows the decision-making tree for a woman.

The necessary and sufficient condition for a woman to get married is expressed as

$$V_2/V_1 > p_2 - p_1. \tag{1}$$

Inequality (1) implies that two forms of gender discrimination affect women's decisions regarding marriage. One is the gender gap in income (or wage); this concerns the left hand side of Inequality (1),

Figure 1.2: The decision-making tree for a woman

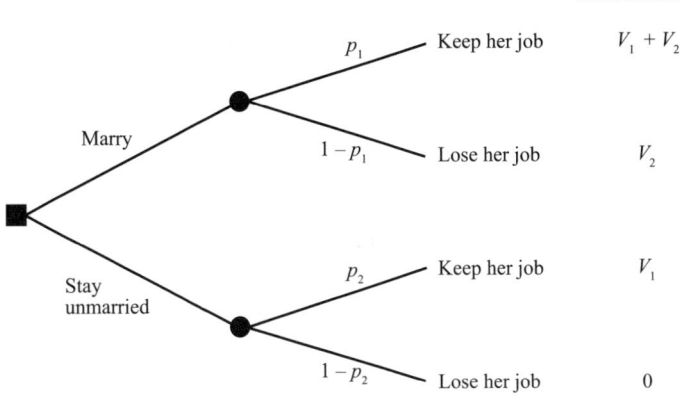

V_1: A woman's own income (if she keeps her job) V_2: A (prospective) husband's income
p_1: P (Keeping her job | Marrying) p_2: P (Keeping her job | Staying unmarried)

that is, V_2/V_1. The other is the 'marriage bar,' that is, the gender-based discrimination that typically takes the form of excluding married women from full-time employment; this concerns the right hand side of Inequality (1), that is, $p_2 - p_1$.

In order to establish a micro–macro link, I introduced the following two assumptions.

• *Assumption 1*: V_1 and V_2 are subject to a log-normal distribution respectively (e.g. Aitchson and Brown 1957; Gibrat 1931).
More formally, $\log V_1 \sim N(\mu_1, \sigma_1)$, and $\log V_2 \sim N(\mu_2, \sigma_2)$.
• *Assumption 2*: A woman is randomly coupled with only one marriage candidate. (There is no other chance for marriage.)

On these assumptions, we obtain a formula for estimating the proportion of unmarried women:

$$P(\text{Unmarried}) = P\{\log V_2 - \log V_1 \leq c\}$$
$$= P\{Z \leq Z_c\},$$

where

$$Z = \frac{(\log V_2 - \log V_1) - (\mu_2 - \mu_1)}{\sqrt{\sigma_1^2 + \sigma_2^2}},$$

$$Z_c = \frac{c - (\mu_2 - \mu_1)}{\sqrt{\sigma_1^2 + \sigma_2^2}},$$

and

$$c = \log(p_2 - p_1). \qquad (2)$$

From this formula, we can deduce three major macro-level predictions as follows.

- *Prediction 1*: The greater the gender gap in average income ($\mu_2 - \mu_1$), the smaller the proportion of unmarried women.
- *Prediction 2*: The more severe the marriage bar ($p_2 - p_1$), the greater the proportion of unmarried women.
- *Prediction 3*: The greater the degree in intra-gender inequality, as measured by the standard deviation of the logarithm of income (σ_1 or σ_2), the greater the proportion of unmarried women, especially in industrial societies entailing the condition $\mu_2 - \mu_1 > c$.

The standard deviation of the logarithm of income is one of the commonly used measures of income inequality (Sen 1997: 28–29). Moreover, it is proved that if we assume a log-normal distribution of income, then the Gini coefficient, another frequently-used measure of income inequality, becomes a function of the standard deviation of the logarithm of income (Aitchson and Brown 1957: 13, Theorem 2.7).

Data and method

Data: official statistics of Japan

The data used for the purposes of this chapter are taken from the following two surveys conducted by the government of Japan.[3] One is the Basic Survey on Wage Structure (Policy Planning and Research Department, Ministry of Labor, Japan, 1965–2005). This survey provides us with frequency tables on income distribution (per month) for full- and part-time employees in total, by gender, and by age group.[4] The other is the Labor Force Survey (Statistical Bureau, Management and Coordination Agency, Japan, 1965–2001; Statistical Bureau, Ministry of Public Management, Home Affairs, Posts and Telecommunications, Japan 2002–2004; Statistical Bureau, Ministry of Internal Affairs and Communications, Japan 2005–2006). This survey provides us with data on the frequency distributions of various types of workers, such as full-time or permanent part-time employees, casual or irregular employees, and self-employed workers. I use the data from these surveys in order to describe the trends in the gender gap in income by age group, the difference in the proportion of full-

or permanent part-time employees between unmarried and married women by age group, and the trend in gender-based income inequality by age group.[5]

Method

On the one hand, I employ the method of quantiles (or percentiles) (Aitchson and Brown 1957: 40–42) instead of ordinary maximum likelihood estimation in order to estimate the mean (μ) and the standard deviation (σ) of a log-normal distribution of wage or income. This is because, for the grouped data published in the reports of the Basic Survey on Wage Structure, not only would the maximum likelihood method become cumbersome as the number of wage categories increases (Aitchson and Brown 1957: 53), but the quantile method also has an advantage of retaining comparability even if the number of categories changes year by year. For every year, the quantile method allows us to estimate the means and standard deviations of wage distributions of the four groups: males aged 25–29, males aged 30–34, females aged 25–29, and females aged 30–34.[6] (See the Appendix for the detail of the method.)

On the other hand, I calculate the proportion of regular employees among unmarried women and that among married women for the two age groups, that is, women aged 25–29 and women aged 30–34, for every year, using data from the Labor Force Survey. The proportion is obtained by dividing the number of regular employees by the total (including the unemployed and those who are not in the labor force).

I use the ratio of the median wage for female regular employees to that for their male counterparts as an index of gender-based wage disparity. As the ratio approaches 1, the gender gap in wage narrows, while as the ratio approaches 0, the gender gap widens. If we observe that the value of the ratio increases over time, the observed trend will provide support for *Prediction 1*.

I also use the difference in the proportion of regular employees among unmarried and married women as an index of the marriage bar. If we can find an increasing trend in the value of the index, the development will support *Prediction 2*.

Inequality within the sexes is measured by the estimated standard deviation of the logarithm of the wage or income. This is because, as I mentioned above, the standard deviation of the logarithm of income is one of the commonly used measures of inequality. If the standard deviation increases over the years, the trend will support *Prediction 3*.

Moreover, I examine the estimated proportions of unmarried women, which are obtained by substituting the estimates for $p_1, p_2, \mu_1, \mu_2, \sigma_1$, and σ_2 into Equation (2), from both quantitative and qualitative analytical perspectives.[7] In other words, on the one hand, I examine the relationship between the estimated proportions of unmarried women and the situation in reality. On the other hand, I ascertain whether the trend in estimated proportions can replicate the trend in actual proportions.

Testing predictions and estimation

Gender wage gap

Figure 1.3 shows the trend in the gender gap in wages in Japan from 1965 to 2005 (cf. Kimura 2010: 158–159). The degree of the gender gap is measured by the ratio of the median wage (per month) of female full-time or regular employees (M_f) to that of their male counterparts (M_m). We can observe that the gender gap in wage has dramatically decreased but not disappeared entirely. The ratio of the median wage for female regular employees aged 25–29 to that for their male counterparts in 1965 was 0.61, while the ratio of the median wage for female full-time or permanent part-time employees aged 25–29 to that for their male counterparts in 2005 was 0.89. The ratio of the median wage for female full-time or permanent part-time employees aged 30–34 to that for their male counterparts in 1965 was 0.49, while the ratio of the median wage for female regular employees aged 30–34 to that for their male counterparts in 2005 was 0.82.

According to *Prediction 1*, the declining gender wage gap would be a force that would increase the proportion of unmarried women. The proportion of unmarried women has in fact increased, in support of *Prediction 1*.

Marriage bar

Contrary to the trend in the gender disparity in wage, the degree of the marriage bar does not seem to have changed. Both the proportion of full-time (or regular) employees among unmarried women and that among married women have gradually increased. Nevertheless, the difference between the proportion of full-time employees among unmarried women and that among married women has only slightly decreased.

Figure 1.3: Gender wage gap (M_f/M_m) for two age groups in Japan, 1965–2005

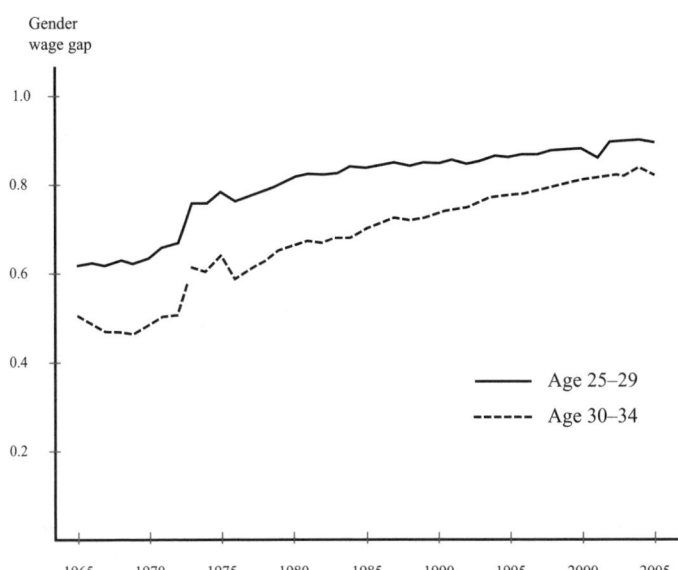

Source: Basic Survey on Wage Structure (Policy Planning and Research Development Department, Ministry of Labor, Japan, 1965–2005).

Note: M_f stands for the median wage of female regular employees and M_m for that of male regular employees. The ratio of M_f/M_m represents the degree of the gender gap in wage.

Figure 1.4 shows the differences between the proportion of regular employees among unmarried women and that among married women (for the trends in the proportions of regular employees, see figures 8.3 and 8.4 in Kimura (2010)). The difference in the proportion for women aged 25–29 in 1968 was 0.52 while that in 2005 was 0.38; the difference in the proportion for women aged 30–34 in 1968 was 0.45 while that in 2005 was 0.36.

These figures reveal that the marriage bar remains in contemporary Japan although, on average, both the proportion of regular employees among unmarried women and that among married women have gradually increased regardless of age group. Generally speaking, the difference in the proportion of regular employees between unmarried and married women has been about 0.4 (40 percentage points).

As for *Prediction 2*, we have two alternative implications. One is that the persisting marriage bar might not affect the proportion of

Figure 1.4: Difference in the proportion of regular employees for unmarried and married women

Source: Labor Force Survey (Statistical Bureau, Management and Coordination Agency, Japan, 1965–2001; Statistical Bureau, Ministry of Public Management, Home Affairs, Posts and Telecommunications, Japan, 2002–2004; Statistical Bureau, Ministry of Internal Affairs and Communications, Japan, 2005–2006).

Note: Data for 1967 are missing. The figures for 1965 and 1966 represent the percentages of employees among unmarried women and married women (aged 25–29).

unmarried women. The other is that the Japanese data itself might be inadequate to test *Prediction 2* because there is little change in the degree of the marriage bar from 1965 through 2005. In any case, no evidence in support of *Prediction 2* was revealed.

In addition, it is worth noting that the difference in the proportions of regular employees between married and unmarried women for both the age groups has begun to decline slightly since 1993, and the trends of the two age groups have become similar since 1998. However, these recent trends are not brought about by the increment in the proportion of married female regular employees but by the decrement in the proportion of unmarried female regular employees. The decrement might be a result of the economic recession following the bubble economy in the 1980s in Japan.

Inequality within the sexes

Figure 1.5 shows the trend in the inequality within the sexes as measured by the standard deviation of the logarithm of income (σ_1 or σ_2), in Japan from 1965 to 2005. Income inequality has dramatically decreased, especially for female regular employees aged 30–34. The standard deviation for female employees aged 30–34 in 1965 was 0.49 while that in 2005 was 0.29. For the other three groups, we observe only moderately decreasing trends in the value of the standard until 2000 (especially from 1965 to 1975) and slightly increasing trends after 2001.

In addition, the gender difference in the degree of inequality was more salient than the age group disparity prior to 1987, while the age group difference in the degree of inequality was more salient than the gender difference post-1988.

These trends suggest that, according to *Prediction 3*, the proportion of unmarried women aged 30–34 should have decreased from 1965 to 2005, while that of women aged 25–29 should have remained

Figure 1.5: Standard deviation of income for regular employees by gender and age group

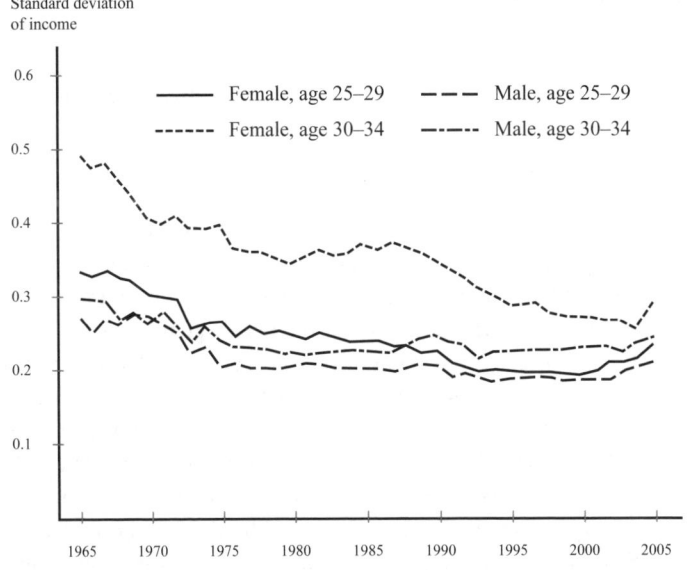

Source: Basic Survey on Wage Structure (Policy Planning and Research Department, Ministry of Labor, Japan, 1965–2005).

relatively stable. However, as we have seen, the proportions of unmarried women in both age groups were growing. Thus, we found evidence that went against *Prediction 3*.

Estimation versus reality

Table 1.1 shows the estimated and actual proportions of unmarried women aged 25–29 and 30–34. We can see that the proportions estimated in terms of my model (Kimura 2000), more specifically speaking, in terms of Equation (2), are very much smaller than the actual proportions. From the quantitative analytical view, the model shows a poor performance. However, from this view, we can observe that the model replicates the increase in the actual proportions of unmarried women of both age groups from 1985 through 1990. Nevertheless, the successful replication is confined to only these periods. Thus, we should conclude that my model published in 2000 is ineffective in both the quantitative and qualitative senses, although the trend in the estimates of the proportion of unmarried women from the model may not be totally wrong.

Concluding remarks

A wrong hypothesis is better than no hypothesis.
———Johann Wolfgang von Goethe

Summary of the results

Frey and Eichenberger (1996) pointed out that empirical evidence deviates from predictions based on the 'rational' view of marriage, and called this fact the 'marriage paradox.' I have to admit that my model (Kimura 2000) is another example of the marriage paradox.

We observed the decreasing gender wage gap as well as the increasing proportions of unmarried women. Thus, *Prediction 1* may be supported. However, we also observed that the marriage bar has persisted in Japan. This means that we cannot find any evidence for *Prediction 2* or that our Japanese data is not adequate to test this forecast. Moreover, the income inequality measured by the standard deviation of logarithm of income has decreased, especially for women aged 30–34. This is opposite to the expected outcome of *Prediction 3*.

What is worse is that the deviation of the estimated proportions of unmarried women from the actual proportions of unmarried women

Table 1.1 Percentages of unmarried women: estimated and actual values

	Age 25–29		Age 30–34	
	Estimated %	**Actual %**	**Estimated %**	**Actual %**
1965	0.24	18.9	0.41	9.0
1966	0.19	–	0.28	–
1967	–	–	–	–
1968	0.36	–	0.28	–
1969	0.25	–	0.15	–
1970	0.31	18.1	0.23	7.2
1971	0.36	–	0.08	–
1972	0.23	–	0.23	–
1973	0.41	–	0.55	–
1974	0.31	–	0.54	–
1975	0.29	20.9	0.44	7.7
1976	0.14	–	0.09	–
1977	0.10	–	0.11	–
1978	0.11	–	0.11	–
1979	0.12	–	0.09	–
1980	0.14	24.0	0.09	9.1
1981	0.23	–	0.07	–
1982	0.17	–	0.06	–
1983	0.09	–	0.08	–
1984	0.11	–	0.08	–
1985	0.15	30.6	0.08	10.4
1986	0.12	–	0.07	–
1987	0.16	–	0.10	–
1988	0.14	–	0.11	–
1989	0.21	–	0.14	–
1990	0.31	40.4	0.21	13.9
1991	0.18	–	0.25	–
1992	0.16	–	0.18	–
1993	0.09	–	0.12	–
1994	0.06	–	0.07	–
1995	0.07	48.2	0.08	19.7
1996	0.04	–	0.08	–
1997	0.05	–	0.07	–
1998	0.02	–	0.04	–
1999	0.01	–	0.03	–
2000	0.01	56.0	0.03	26.6
2001	0.01	–	0.01	–
2002	0.01	–	0.02	–
2003	0.01	–	0.01	–
2004	0.01	–	0.02	–
2005	0.02	59.0	0.03	32.0

Note: The estimates for 1967 cannot be calculated as data on the proportions of female regular employees for the two age groups are missing.

is salient for every year measured. The estimation cannot replicate the actual trend of the proportions of unmarried women, except for the periods from 1985 through 1990. To sum up, there is little empirical support for my model of marriage (Kimura 2000).

Discussion

What is wrong with my model of marriage? I already noted that this model sacrifices reality for simplicity at least in the following four respects (Kimura 2000: 380). First, the model neglects a man's decision-making processes and the negotiations between a man and a woman. Second, it postulates only one opportunity for marriage and the random matching of men and women, although the opportunity may not be limited to one instance and differential association based on such factors as social class and ethnicity typically come into play. Third, it also postulates that the domain of a woman's utility is restricted to income. Finally, it neglects the possibility that married women who have quit their jobs re-enter the labor market (and often do so as part-time workers).

We could continue the list. The expected value model may be inadequate to grasp a real woman's decision-making processes. This is because the model does not take into account some important elements of marital decision-making such as risk, imperfect information, perception of probability, and timing. Moreover, the assumption of log-normal distributions of income is also unrealistic. In fact, Kono (2006) argues that an inverted gamma distribution is more realistic than a log-normal one for describing income distribution. However, for the moment, I hesitate to modify my model because such modification would lead to further complication and less productivity in the sense that it would yield simple and counterintuitive predictions.

There are also difficulties in the method for testing the predictions and estimations derived from the model. In particular, the Basic Survey of Wage Structure has collected mainly data of those who fit the image of employees enjoying the Japanese long-term employment system (see Note 4). Moreover, the survey has not collected data of employees who work in establishments with less than five regular employees (or less than ten regular employees for some years). These two restrictions could cause not only an upward bias in the estimate of the mean wage but also a downward bias in that of the standard deviation of wage. These biases could have contributed to the discrepancy between the estimated and actual proportions of unmarried women.

My final comment: among the difficulties I pointed out above, I think that disregarding the possibility of becoming irregular workers (more specifically, part-time or dispatched workers) is the most crucial factor from the perspective of the increasing diversity of women's life courses as well. This is because some welcome this kind of diversification among women as it would supposedly promote the aggregate level of women's satisfaction, while others regard it as a result of discrimination against women.[8] I believe that satisfaction does not legitimate the *status quo*, because sociological and social psychological studies have already reported the 'relative gratification' among the discriminated and the disadvantaged (e.g. Crosby 1982; Runciman 1966).

Acknowledgment

This study was financially supported by the Japan Economic Research Foundation and the Grant-in-Aid for Scientific Research (Exploratory Research) No.15653028 'Academic Resource Study' (Principal Investigator: Junsuke Hara).

Appendix: Estimation of mean and standard deviation

On the assumption of a log-normal distribution such that $\log V \sim N(\mu, \sigma)$, we can estimate μ and σ as follows:

$$\mu = \ln M$$

and

$$\sigma = \ln\left\{\frac{1}{2}\left(\frac{M}{P_{16}} + \frac{P_{84}}{M}\right)\right\}$$

where M stands for the median and P_x stands for the x-th percentile (Aitchson and Brown 1957: 32).

2 Single Mothers and Child Support Policies in Japan

Miyuki Shimoebisu

Introduction

As the divorce rate in Japan increases, so too, as everywhere, does the number of single mother households. A source of concern in this situation is the high level of poverty among these households.[1] Employment levels for Japanese single mothers are extremely high, but atypical forms of employment are the norm and households are concentrated in the lower-income demographic. A dependent children's allowance (*jidō fuyō teate*) is paid to low-income single mothers, but since the latter half of the 1980s, the level of benefits has been reduced.

Besides employment and welfare benefits, in the case of divorce, paternal child support payments form another possible source of income for single mother households. Many fathers, however, do not pay child support. In the context of the problems of single mother households, in comparison to work issues and welfare benefits there is little discussion on the issue of child support, and society's interest in this regard could not be described as high. Households headed by divorced mothers are nevertheless increasing, and the problem of paternal non-payment is thus predicted to become more serious.

This chapter focuses on the issue of non-payment of child support after divorce and compares policies that address the problem in Japan with those of five western nations.[2] From there, the features of Japanese policy are identified, and the nature of future child support policies is discussed.

The realities of child support

After divorce, as during marriage, parents have an obligation to maintain their children. A father who lives away from his children is therefore required to fulfill this obligation by paying child support. In the event of divorce, child support is determined by consultation

Table 2.1: Divorced single mothers and child support (%)

	Continue to receive child support	Have received child support	Have never received child support	Unknown
1983	11.3	10.1	78.6	–
1988	14.0	10.6	75.4	–
1993	14.9	16.4	68.7	–
1998	20.8	16.4	60.1	–
2003	17.7	15.4	66.8	–
2006	19.0	16.0	59.1	5.9

Source: Ministry of Health, Labor and Welfare, Zenkoku Boshi Setai tō Chōsa (National Survey of Single Mother and Other Households) (1983, 1988, 1993, 1998, 2003, 2006).

between the parties, but where agreement cannot be reached, or where consultation is not possible, the Family Court makes a determination.

Notwithstanding, determinations concerning child support are not compulsory, and there is no system for examining whether or not a divorced couple has determined child support, or whether the nature of the outcome is appropriate. For this reason, approximately 85% of divorces established in the Family Court involve a determination,[3] but in cases of divorce by mutual agreement—approximately 90% of cases—most couples divorce without a determination being made.

In such circumstances, therefore, few households headed by divorced mothers actually receive child support. Table 2.1 illustrates the results of a survey conducted by the Ministry of Health, Labor and Welfare. The figures show that the rate of receipt of child support by households headed by divorced mothers rose from 11.3% in 1983, but that the figure has been stalled at around 20% since the late 1990s and was at 19% in 2006. A 2009 survey conducted by an organization for single mothers found that the proportion of single mothers regularly receiving child support was 21%: 80% of fathers were not properly paying child support. There were two reasons for non-payment reported (by mothers) in almost equal proportion: '(the father) does not consider the obligation for child support to be that of the parent' (32%), and 'lack of economic capacity' (33%) (National Federation of Single Parents and Children's Welfare Associations 2009).

In this way, non-payment of child support has become the norm. The problem is not only with the capacity of fathers to pay; it also concerns their willingness to contribute in this regard.

Child support policy

Current systems

The systems a single mother can access in order to secure unpaid child support are the Family Court System to Secure Performance (*Katei Saibansho Rikōu Kakuho Seido*) and the Civil Enforcement System (*Kyōsei Shikkō Seido*). Both are judicial systems. In the Family Court System if an obligation decided by the Family Court is not fulfilled, a performance notice or order is issued. Even when a child support decision goes unfulfilled, a mother can apply for a performance notice or order. The application is cheap, and the process is easy, but the system can only be used in cases where the Family Court has decided child support. The system also has the problem of being weak on enforceability. A performance notice requires spontaneous payment by the father, but there is no punishment if he does not respond. A performance order is a legal measure that is a step up in strength. However, even if the order is not obeyed, nothing more than an administrative fine of less than 100,000 yen accrues.

Where there is a Family Court decision about child support, or the content of the determination is drawn up in a notarized deed, the Civil Enforcement System can be used to seize a father's salary or savings. Many single mothers want monthly seizure of wages to ensure regular child support. In order to actually make such an application, confirmation of the father's address, place of work and income status are required. After divorce it is often the case that contact with the other party lapses, and it is not always easy to collect information on the father. There are also problems with the legal process. Appointing a lawyer is so costly that, in reality, there are few single mother households able to access the system. In addition, if the father leaves his place of employment, the procedures must be followed again from scratch.

Securing child support also became an issue in welfare policy for single mother households, and in October 2007 the national government opened the Child Support Counseling and Assistance Centre. The centre provides telephone or email counseling about child support, and enquiries to these are on the rise. However, the centre only provides indirect support through general information or advice and is unable to provide more direct assistance, such as negotiating with a father or collecting child support.

It is therefore apparent that in practical terms, both systems can be described as inaccessible to most single mother households and even if mothers are able to use the systems, their effectiveness cannot be relied upon. Article 27.4 of the United Nations Convention on the Rights of the Child states 'Parties shall take all appropriate measures to secure the recovery of maintenance for the child from the parents or other persons having financial responsibility for the child, both within the State Party and from abroad.' Japan ratified the Convention in 1994 and the Japanese Government has reported to the United Nations that the Article has been addressed by the aforementioned prevailing systems. It is nevertheless clear that the current systems are far from an adequate set of measures.

Historical perspective

Society's level of interest in the issue of child support cannot be described as high, but in the debate on the dependent children's allowance, the obligation of the father to maintain the child is cited as grounds for reducing benefits. Dependent children's allowances are welfare benefits paid to low-income households headed by divorced mothers. The allowances have been paid since 1962, but with the number of recipients growing, multiple systemic reforms have reduced benefits since the latter half of the 1980s. Non-payment of child support has been repeatedly identified as a problem by the reform agenda, and the need for measures to address the issue has been debated. Among the reforms were two opportunities that can be considered turning points for child support policy.

The first was a suggestion in the Divorce System Research Report (*Rikon Seido tō Kenkyūkai Hōkokusho*) published in December 1985. In 1985 benefits were slashed as a result of major reforms to the dependent children's allowance system. The *Rikon Seido tō Kenkyūkai* was a research body established as a private advisory group to the Minister for Health and Welfare to work toward systemic reforms. The team was comprised of experts and investigated problems with Japanese child support and a range of overseas child support systems. The group's report clearly described the results of investigations and ultimately suggested the introduction of a system for collecting paternal child support payments. The system was one in which, for cases where a dependent children's allowance was being paid, the government could bill fathers, and funds collected from them could be applied to recouping benefits.

Before the group's report was submitted, however, the Revised Dependent Children's Allowance Law was enacted and thereafter, because the number of benefit recipients declined, the research group's suggestions were not considered. In essence, the government's focus of interest was on controlling public payments, and measures to address the question of child support after divorce were not undertaken. Around the same time, welfare payments and non-payment of child support to single mother households also emerged as problems in the US and the UK, and in both countries a system of child support was put in place. In Japan, however, it was only cuts to benefits that were implemented.

The second opportunity to address the issue arose in 1997 when the government took a practical look at introducing a system for collecting costs from fathers. The amount paid in the dependent children's allowance had been curtailed by the revision of the system in 1985, and debate had died down. But thereafter the number of recipients again rose, and the discussion on reducing benefits was reignited. In that context, in 1997 a child welfare advisory group suggested that a system for collecting costs from fathers be introduced for cases of recipients of the dependent children's allowance. The same suggestion had been made after a ten-year hiatus following the release of the 1985 report. The Ministry of Health and Welfare, which had been pushed by fiscal authorities to control benefits, this time began investigating a system and moved to implementation. However, introduction was foregone at the point at which negotiations were entered into with the then ruling party (the Liberal Democratic Party). The reasoning was said to be as follows: the obligation for a father to pay child support post-divorce required amendments under Civil Law, so it was surmised that the backlash from conservative politicians would be severe in response to the government becoming directly involved in the divorce issue. It was through this process that the introduction of a system of cost collection was frustrated at the investigation stage, and ever since, the government has been unforthcoming about policies that directly address the issue of child support. In this way, the opportunity for major policy reform, in the form of the introduction of new systems, failed to occur, and to the present day the debate on child support policy has been at a standstill (Shimoebisu 2008).

Child support policy in Europe and America

Non-payment of child support is a problem that is not unique to Japan. The rate of receipt of child support in several countries is shown in Table 2.2.

Table 2.2: Single parents receiving child support (%)

	1994	2000	2004
Sweden	85.4	92.6	100.0
Germany	n.a.	30.1	n.a.
France	55.9	46.3	n.a.
USA	28.8	34.1	33.7
UK	20.2	21.9	22.8

Source: OECD Family Database, Table PF5.2 (2010).

Receipt levels in Sweden are perfect, but this is due—as will be discussed below—to the Swedish system of benefits. Table 2.2 also shows that all the countries have issues with non-payment of child support. That said, compared to the rate of receipt of child support in Japan (Table 2.1), rates in these countries are higher. Analysis of individual policies shows that in addition to the judicial system, the various countries have implemented systems to secure child support.[4] The nature of the system differs from country to country, but in all cases the problem of child support is the direct responsibility of a welfare bureaucracy.

Sweden

In Sweden, if child support is not paid, a child support supplementary benefit (*underhållsstöd*) is contributed. This is basically an advance for maintenance and has been in effect since 1937. The detail of the system has changed since the 1940s with requirements in relation to payment being gradually eased, and currently it applies broadly to parents in general.

Where child support is not paid, the social insurance office pays a child support supplementary benefit to the mother until the child becomes 18 years old. Thereafter, the social insurance office claims an obligatory payment from the father and the monies collected are applied to recouping the benefit. The amount of the benefit in 2010 was the minimum guaranteed child support as determined by the national government, set at 1273 SEK per child per month.

The amount a father is obliged to pay is calculated as a fixed percentage of the father's income, but generous reductions and exclusions are available, depending on the father's circumstances. In particular, since the 1970s policies have sought 'care rather than cash' from the father; in other words, the emphasis has been on interaction with the child rather than economic support (Bergman and Hobson 2002).

There are no limits placed on the mother's income affecting the receipt of benefits. In other words, benefits are paid even if a mother living with a child has a high income. The income of the child itself (income from assets or the like) is subject to restrictions. In addition, even if the mother remarries or lives with a new partner, the benefit payment continues.

In this way, Sweden has a policy by which the nation effectively fulfils the responsibility to support children. Here the emphasis is on the protection of the rights of the child.

Germany

In Germany, as is the case in Sweden, when a father does not pay child support an advance is paid for child support maintenance (*unterhaltsvorschuss*). This has been in effect since 1980. The Youth Welfare Office (*jugendamt*) pays benefits to the mother, and thereafter the office bills the father. The monies collected are applied to recouping the benefit. The amount of the benefit is set on the basis of a standard rate for maintenance determined by the national government, and in 2010 this was 133 Euros per month per child aged zero to five, and 180 Euros for children aged six to 11.

As in Sweden, there is no limit on the mother's income that affects receipt of the benefit. However, in Germany the period of payment is restricted, and benefit payments are designed to support children aged below 12 for a maximum of six years. Further, unlike Sweden, if the mother remarries or lives with a new partner, benefit payment ceases.

In other words, for children in single parent households, Germany has a policy by which the nation guarantees maintenance of the child. The nature of the policy is that of economic aid until the circumstances of a single mother household stabilize.

France

In the same way in France, when child support is not paid, a family support benefit (*Allocation de Soutien Familial: ASF*) is paid from a family benefit fund (*Caisse Allocations Familiales: CAF*). The CAF is a public institution that handles France's various types of family payments. The ASF is an expansion to the divorced, of the orphan benefit originally paid only on separation by death, and has been in force since 1985. In the case of divorce, once the CAF has paid the benefit it is recovered from the father and the monies collected are applied to recouping benefits. The value of benefits in 2010 was 87.14 Euros per month per child.

In France also the benefit is not limited by the mother's income. However, there are conditions on the mother's ability to apply for the benefit, in that she must advise the court of non-fulfillment of a child support order for over two months. As in Germany, if the mother remarries or lives with a new partner, the benefit is no longer paid.

As a result, in France the policy is for the national government to guarantee child support for children in single parent households, supplementing the function of the courts.

The US

The United States has a coercive system in which government institutions collect child support from fathers who do not pay. The background to the introduction of this system was criticism of the handling of child support under the judicial system. The criticism hinges on three main issues. First, there was no consistency in decisions on child support by judicial discretion. Second, the judicial process costs time and money. Finally, in the event that payments were not made in contravention of a judgment, enforcement measures were inadequate.

In response, in 1975 a national system of child support was implemented, wherein the Federal Government established the Office of Child Support Enforcement, and an authority responsible for child support was established in each state. The nature of the system varies from state to state, but federal legislation achieves uniformity, and there are four main programs in place, as outlined below.
1. Locating Non-Custodial Parents. Both federal and state authorities operate a parent location service, and the responsible child support agencies are afforded powerful rights of gathering relevant information.
2. Establishing Paternity. To enable unmarried mothers to quickly establish paternity, both a process of voluntary acknowledgement and genetic testing are used.
3. Establishing Support Orders. In order to avoid dispute at the determination stage, all states have legislated guidelines enabling specific calculation of child support levels.

4. Collecting Support. Enforcement measures have been strengthened particularly since the latter half of the 1980s. The measures include deductions from wages, refund of income tax and offsets from unemployment benefits. There are also indirect means of enforcement in place, such as defaulters having their driving license or occupational licenses suspended, or being refused the issue of a passport. If the father still does not make payment, legal sanctions are imposed, and in addition, there are social sanction measures such as the issuance of posters that represent the defaulter as a criminal.

The system may be used by anyone. Single mother households in receipt of public assistance, however, are legally subject to the system, and the mother is obliged to cooperate. Enforcement may be waived if there has been incidence of domestic violence or other similar justified reasons. However, the system is criticized for the failure of waiver stipulations to function.

Child support collected by states from fathers is applied to recouping payments in cases where mothers are receiving public assistance, and are paid to mothers in cases where public assistance is not received. In the latter case, the child support system becomes an agency service for the mothers in which child support is secured through a public institution.

In this way in the US government agencies are actively involved in the child support issue, but no benefits are paid in advance. For that reason, the US policy is one in which the government pursues parents and aggressively enforces payments.

The UK

The United Kingdom was traditionally lenient in the matter of pursuing a father's responsibilities to maintain children after divorce. In the final stages of the conservative administration in the 1980s, however, the reliance on welfare of single mother households and non-payment of child support emerged as issues and a government child support system was introduced. The background to this situation, as in the US debate, was criticism that the court system was contributing to paternal irresponsibility.

The Child Support Agency was established in 1991, and locating the abode of fathers and determination and collection of child support have been implemented since 1993. US methods are used, such as legislating calculation guidelines and deductions from wages and suspension of various licenses. In the case of the UK system, however, since the outset, delays and errors in case management have been rife and criticism of the system has been harsh, precipitating repeated system modifications.

The system can be used by anyone. Traditionally, as in the US, single mothers receiving public assistance were forced to be subject to the system. As of October 2008 in the UK, however, enforcement on recipients of public assistance was scrapped and the system was revised to voluntary use. Improvements have also been made in recent years in the child support collected. Originally in cases where public assistance was being received, funds collected were applied to recouping payments, but that was severely criticized for the fact that, even if a father paid child support, this did not lead to improvements in the circumstances of impoverished households headed by single mothers. As of April 2010, therefore, in cases of recipients of public assistance the full amount of child support collected from the father is paid to the mother, as is the case for single mother households not receiving assistance. Just as in the US, however, in the UK benefits are not paid in advance.

In contrast, in 2008 a separate new system was introduced. The system is one that respects and assists determinations and payments agreed between the parties. The government has established the Child Maintenance and Enforcement Commission, which since October 2008 has provided an information service pertaining to child support decisions and payments for cases that do not use the child support system run by the aforementioned Child Support Agency. The intent is to endeavor to reduce cases of use of the child support system and the burden of system operation.

In this way the UK's system has undergone frequent reforms, all of which have been aimed at improving the efficiency of the government's child support system. At this current stage, therefore, at the core of the UK child support policy is a system of government enforcement of payments.

Features of Japan: an international comparison

Advances for maintenance and the government's child support system

There are two approaches apparent in the child maintenance policies of the above five nations. One is payment of advances for maintenance, and the other is a government child support system.

Advances for maintenance are available in Sweden, Germany and France. Despite being an 'advance,' recovery rates from fathers are very low. According to Skinner et al. (2007), the recovery rates in Germany, France and Sweden are 15%, 22%, and 49%, respectively. There is nevertheless no discussion of scrapping or reducing benefits. This is probably because in these countries there is a well-established range of benefits for families raising children, and because the reality is that the citizens of these countries accept advances for maintenance that may become payments to single mothers. Thus advances for maintenance are a policy tending toward state guaranteed maintenance of children, typified by the Swedish system.

Systems of government child support are in place in the US and the UK. In both countries the intent in introducing the systems was to recover welfare benefits to single mother households from fathers, but the reality is that the fiscal burden of operating the system is significant. Investigation of revenue and expenditure under the US system reveals that government expenditure far exceeds funds collected from fathers resulting in fiscal deficit. The system is maintained and continues in spite of this problem probably because the value of family self-help is widely imbued in the people. This type of child support system is a policy that tends toward state pursuit of the father's responsibility for maintenance, typified by the US system.

The Scandinavian and Anglo Saxon models

The two approaches of state guarantee of maintenance and pursuit of paternal responsibility for maintenance correspond to J. Millar's (1996) two models of child support policy. Millar broadly classifies child support policies into the Scandinavian and Anglo Saxon models. Millar's models were used as the basis for an investigation of the Swedish and US systems, and the characteristics of both are as summarized in Table 2.3.

The Scandinavian model is typified by the Swedish child support assistance system, which may be deemed state guaranteed maintenance of children. Allowances are in the nature of advance payment of child support by the state, but given that recovery rates are low, in real terms the policy may be described as a 'family benefit model.' In this model, public maintenance of children takes precedence over private maintenance, and the philosophy underpinning the policy is that children and child rearing belong to the public domain. The

Table 2.3: Two child support policy models

	Scandinavian model	Anglo Saxon model
Typical system	Sweden's child support benefits (advances for maintenance, since 1937)	America's child support system (since 1975)
National response to issue of child support	State guarantee of child support	Sate purusit of parental responsibility for care
Type of child support policy	Family benefit model	Family intervention model
Attitude to maintenance of children	Public maintenance > Private maintenance	Public maintenance < Private maintenance
Underlying view of children	Public nature of children and child raising	Private nature of children and child raising
Image of father in child support policy	Breadwinner ≤ Carer	Breadwinner
Policy attitude to separated fathers	Broad-minded	Punitive
Family ideology emphasised	Principle of family love	Principle of family self-help
Relationship to family policy	Consistent	Consistent
References		
Family image underpinning family policy	Family in which both parents work and share child raising	Family that is self-supporting in the market
Father image in family policy	Breadwinner = Carer	Breadwinner
Father image in child support policy	Breadwinner ≤ Carer	Breadwinner

policy seeks economic support and interaction with the child by the father, in other words the roles of both breadwinner and carer. In the event that the father is unable to fulfill both roles, however, the policy is generous to the father and gives precedence to the carer role over the breadwinner role. It may be described as a policy that applies the principle of modern family love to divorced parents and children.

The Anglo Saxon model is typified by the American child support system, which may be deemed state pursuit of parental responsibility. As a type of policy it is a 'family intervention model' in which private maintenance of children takes precedence over public maintenance. Underpinning the model is the belief that children and child rearing are ultimately private matters. The policy is punitive against fathers, seeking the breadwinner role irrespective of circumstances. It is a policy that applies the principle of modern family self-help to divorced parents and children.

Family policies and child support policies

We will now turn to the perspectives of family policies versus those of child support policies. Family policy is a polysemic concept, but Shoji Yoko defines family policies as 'individual policies which are formulated and implemented by a state, or a local government or other policy-making entity that have the intent of achieving a particular effect on families, or the collective of those measures,' and says that the objective of such policies is 'to place families in general in the situation that the policy-making entity considers desirable' (Shoji 1999: 136–7). In other words, the design of a family policy is based on a certain family image. Then by comparing the image of the father of a family that is the basis for family policy and that of the father in child support policy, we could identify a relationship between child support policy and family support policy.

In Sweden the principle of gender equality underpins a system of parental leave and public childcare services. The family image behind this type of family policy is that of a family in which both parents work and share child rearing. The image of the father in that model is of both breadwinner and carer. This is almost the same as the image of the father in the child support policy examined above. In that sense the child support policy is congruent with the family policy.

Conversely, the US is the only country among the advanced nations that does not have a system of child benefits, and parental leave is limited. Public childcare services are also targeted at impoverished households, and at the heart of childcare policy is a system of tax deductions for the cost of parental purchase of private childcare services. The family image that underpins the US family policy is that of a family that is self-supporting in the market and not reliant on welfare. The image of the father is that of breadwinner, which is congruent with the image of the father in child support policy. In this sense child support policy is congruent with family policy in the US, too.

As evident from the above, the Scandinavian and Anglo Saxon models contrast significantly in terms of the way issue of child support is addressed, and the policy measures and images of the father that underpin policy. However, what is as important as this is that both models are congruent with their respective family policies. In other words, these child support policies seek to bring father and child in the post-divorce situation closer to the same status as father and child in the two-parent family model, which is considered desirable by the policy-making entity. In short, the child support policies of the Scandinavian and Anglo Saxon models are continuations of their respective family policies.

The two models and Japan

Japan has neither an advance for maintenance allowances nor a government system of child support. As can be seen from the process of cutting the dependent children's allowance, in relation also to the maintenance of children, private care takes precedence. There is a strong view that children and child rearing are private matters, and the emphasis is thus on family self-help.

Japan shares these basic principles with the Anglo Saxon model. However, for fathers who fail to fulfill their responsibilities to maintain their children after divorce, there has been a dearth of policy that addresses the issue, and fathers who do not fulfill these obligations are left alone. In so far as the child support issue is concerned, the view that government should not intervene in family matters is firmly entrenched. This is decidedly at odds with the value system represented in the Anglo Saxon model.

With respect to Japanese family policy, declining birth rates have been the background to progress in support of child rearing since the 1990s. In particular, policy support for families in which both parents work are well established in the form of public childcare and parental leave, and support has recently become available for fathers to encourage them to take parental leave. A closer look into the detail of the system, however, reveals that parenting by mothers is the norm and that the policy has not escaped the hegemonic family model in which labor is divided along gender lines. In other words, a family in the system is assumed to be one in which the father is the breadwinner and the mother is the carer and perhaps the secondary breadwinner.

In this way, the image of the father in Japan's family policy is definitely that of breadwinner. Conversely, as discussed so far, the view of the father in child support policy is obscure. The intent of policy-making entities as to the situation they are seeking to place the father and child in after divorce is unclear. In short, there is a discrepancy between Japan's child support policy and its family policy.

Conclusion

In Japan, as shown above, child support policy fails as family policy. The father and child after divorce fall outside the scope of family policy. Put another way, Japan's family policy applies only to two-parent families. Divorce is on the rise and living in a household headed by a single mother has become a relatively commonplace experience. In family policy based on a two-parent family model, however, households headed by single mothers face difficult circumstances. In the background to low incomes and poverty among single mother households are not only the problems of policy in relation to working women and welfare, but also the issue of the absence of child support policy as family policy. As part of a package of social support afforded to single mother households, Japan also needs policy that ensures government child support.

Should Japan then move towards one of the two models outlined above, the Scandinavian or the Anglo Saxon model? From the perspective of child welfare, the Scandinavian model, in which the state guarantees maintenance irrespective of the father's attitude, is desirable. At this stage, however, introducing the Scandinavian family payment model to Japan is impractical and unfeasible. This is because there is only a short history in Japan of cash payments to children and to families with children. OECD data on public payments to families as a proportion of GDP (in 2003) show that compared to 1.6% in Sweden, Japan managed a mere 0.3% (OECD 2007). In Japan's social environment, it would be politically difficult to introduce advances for maintenance for households headed by divorced mothers.

If a system were to be introduced to Japan, it is highly likely that Japan would aim for the Anglo Saxon model, as there is much thinking in common about the maintenance of children. But the US child support system, which typifies that model, has both advantages and disadvantages. Through this system, single mother households not receiving public assistance are able to avoid the challenges of direct negotiation with fathers, and the system is effective as a public service in which child support is assured. Having parents free from divorce disputes is also an advantage for children.

Conversely, for single mother households receiving public assistance, the above is a dangerous system that threatens the household's subsistence. Households headed by single mothers are subject to enforcement under the system, and mothers deemed by the system to be uncooperative experience restrictions on their public assistance payments. For victims of domestic violence who have justifiable reasons, the obligation to cooperate is waived, but there are few women able to prove they are victims of this crime. Already in the US it is the case that the women in greatest need are those who are deprived of public assistance by the restrictive child support system.

Mothers in single mother households are a minority group in a weak social position. As a form of social support for households headed by single mothers, Japan must introduce a system of government child support. Conceptualization of such a system must be sensitive to and factor in the minority status of mothers in single mother households.

3 Women's Roles and Gender Order in Early Modern and Modern Japan

Rumi Matsuzaki

Introduction

One of the effective approaches for studying the characteristics and structure of various gender gap problems and the significance and issues of postwar reforms in Japan is to elucidate the actual conditions and contexts of the formative process of '*ie*' (corporate household, family: patriarchal lasting social unit which has a family name, homestead, and business), family, and gender order from a historical viewpoint. This chapter explicates the reality of women's roles and gender order in early modern and modern Japan from a historical perspective, examines the continuity and changes from early modern times to modern times, and analyzes the social mechanisms underpinning them.

Japan's social structure in pre-modern (early modern) times or the Edo period can be summarized as follows. Japan's early modern society was a feudal one under samurai government. In other words, the Tokugawa shogunate, headed by a shogun from the Tokugawa clan, was the central government under which provincial lords, called '*daimyō*,' functioned as local governments and ruled their respective territories ('*han*' or domains). There were 260 to 270 domains throughout the country. Edo castle in the city of Edo was the seat of the shogunate government and the residence of the shogun. Provincial *daimyōs* also kept residences in Edo and spent alternate years in the city and their own domains. The samurai class occupied the highest social class, with the remainder of the population belonging to various classes such as peasants, artisans, and merchants.

The samurai society was based on a gendered division of labor denoted by the distinction between *omote* and *oku*. The concepts of *omote* and *oku* were used with regard to spaces within a castle or residence as well as to indicate the way gender roles were divided. The *omote* was an official space in which men conducted politics and the *oku* was a private space in which the feudal lord's family lived their private lives (domestic space). These were clearly separated spaces, and access was strictly controlled at the boundary between them.

As the political power was transferred from the Tokugawa shogunate to the Meiji government in 1867, the nation moved from early modern times into modern times. *Daimyōs* returned their feudal territories and subjects to the Meiji Emperor in 1869. They were appointed as modern domain governors to continue to manage their former territories. At the same time, the Meiji government classified the entire population into four family classes: imperial, noble, samurai (former samurais in general), and commoner (peasants, artisans and merchants) classes. The noble class consisted of former upper court nobles, *daimyōs*, and men who had rendered distinguished services to the state, and the class enjoyed privileged status. This group formed the upper stratum of the national hierarchy. With the abolition of domains and the establishment of prefectures in 1871, former *daimyōs* were dismissed from their domain governor's offices and replaced by government-appointed prefectural governors. This marked the substantial abolishment of the feudal regime and the establishment of nationwide direct rule by the central government.

Since they were unable to participate in politics in the early modern Edo society, women have rarely been addressed as the subject of study on political and social histories. Women's documents have very rarely been examined, as historical materials for analysis have mostly been confined to correspondence between men. The advancement of research on women's history during the 1980s cast some light on topics such as women's property, succession, status, and marriage. Some scholars began to incorporate the concept of gender into their studies from the 1990s (e.g. Nagano 1990; Walthall 2001). In recent years, there have been an increasing number of studies on the women and *oku* affairs of the shogun, *daimyō* and vassal families (e.g. Matsuo 2008; Fukuda 2005; Sugano 2008), and some advancements have been made in research on women in the commoner class and gender issues (e.g. Aoki 2008; Nagashima 2009).

However, there are some problems with these preceding studies. A majority of them focus on the analysis of women in the context of institutions such as laws and the organization of female vassals, and thus the body of research on the actual conditions of women's roles and gender divisions is still small. Study periods tend to be limited, and historical materials for analysis are also confined to certain documents and journals of the *oku*. There are many individual studies on different social classes in various study periods and locations, but their findings need to be positioned and reinterpreted in the context of early modern society. It is also necessary to investigate the macro-level institutional effects on the micro-level actual conditions.

In order to solve these problems, it is necessary to analyze historical materials involving women, compare different social classes, and examine these factors diachronically from early modern times through to modern times. This chapter therefore presents a comparative analysis of women's status and roles, marriage, and the gender system from the early modern period to the beginning of the modern period. Examining the situation of the ruling samurai class and the commoner peasant class, this chapter discusses the characteristics of social stratification at that time, the continuity and changes during the transition from early modern to modern, and their social contexts and factors.

Study subject and approach

The area and family addressed in this analysis are the Satsuma domain and the Shimazu family. During early modern times, the Satsuma domain was the second largest domain at the time situated in southern Japan and covered present-day Kagoshima, Okinawa, and a part of Miyazaki prefectures. The Shimazu family was the ruler (feudal lord) of the Satsuma domain from the end of the 12th to the 19th century. They have been chosen as the study subjects because the territory and ruler were unchanged from early modern times to the beginning of modern times (the Meiji period), and many extant historical materials are available for examination on this subject.

A majority of preceding studies on the women of the Shimazu family in early modern Satsuma concentrate on the period around the establishment of the shogunate and domain system of government (the medieval-early modern transition period), the middle of the early modern period when the adopted daughter of a Tokugawa shogun married into the Shimazu family, and the late early modern period when a Shimazu daughter married into the Tokugawa family (Nagano 1989, 1990; Ego 1998; Yamamoto 2005 and others). These earlier studies also analyze limited groups of historical materials, such as journals of the *oku* in the Satsuma domain and documents written by female vassals working in *oku*. It is envisaged that the various findings of the past that were presented from limited viewpoints can be considered within the context of the shogunate and domain politics and society by diachronically analyzing official communications and political documents of the *omote* in comparison with documents written by women in *oku* setting and interpreting the results in a coherent manner.

While there is a dearth of historical materials that give us a glimpse into the actual conditions of the commoner class in early modern times, some studies have attempted to glean the details of the lives of commoner women and families from historical materials of commendations for good conduct. Sugano (1999, 2001) refers to some cases from the Satsuma domain in her analysis of *Kankoku kōgi roku* (Official records of the acts of dutiful devotion),[1] which is a nationwide collection of commended cases of good conduct compiled by the Tokugawa shogunate. Mega (2008) has examined the cases of commendations for good conduct recorded in the Okayama domain. Since there are no studies that deal specifically with the Satsuma domain, this chapter will attempt to elucidate the daily lives of the commoner people of Satsuma drawing from the aforementioned *Kankoku kōgi roku* and some archival materials of commendations for good conduct compiled in modern times.

The Shimazu family's status was changed from *daimyō* in early modern times to nobility in modern times. While women of the nobility have been studied by Morioka (2002) from a family history viewpoint and the real conditions of noble women in general centering on their relationships with the imperial family have been examined by Otabe (2006, 2007), there have been no specific studies on the *ie*, family, and the actual living conditions of women of the Shimazu family. It is therefore important to clarify the family system of the Shimazu family, outline the actual conditions of their family life, and discuss the way women's roles and gender order within their *ie* changed over time in relation to political and social shifts.

With regard to the early modern ruling class (the Shimazu family),[2] analysis has been carried out on *Shimazu shi seitō keizu* (The orthodox family tree of the Shimazu clan)[3] and *Kansei chōshū shokafu* (The Kansei edition of a compendium of genealogies of *daimyōs* and retainers)[4] as well as historical materials and letters relating to domain administration contained in the *Kyūki zatsuroku* (Collection of historical materials of the Shimazu family and the Satsuma domain)[5] and *Shimazu ke monjo* (Shimazu family documents),[6] including exchanges between women. Analysis has been carried out on historical materials from early modern to modern times of people commended for their good deeds[7] with regard to the early modern commoner class; on *Shimazu shi seitō keizu,* a floor plan of the family residence,[8] memoirs written by a head of the family in modern times,[9] and the family precepts in the Meiji and Taishō periods;[10] and on a supplementary reader at a girls' high school[11] with regard to the establishment of modern gender roles and women in the samurai family in early modern times.

Women's roles and gender order in the early modern ruling class

Roles and marriage of the women of the samurai family

Roles of the legitimate wife
The legitimate wife (officially wedded wife) of a feudal lord lived in a samurai residence in Edo instead of alternating between Edo and the domain with her husband. Her roles included raising and naming the family's children, participating in the life-stage ceremonies of the family such as marriage rituals, holding Buddhist services for deceased feudal lords, praying to Shinto and Buddhist deities for the family and the clan, and engaging in gift-giving rituals with vassals. Many of the feudal lords had concubines (illegitimate wives) in addition to their shogunate-registered legitimate wife and had many children by these women. The legitimate wife became the foster mother of these illegitimate children and raised them as if they were her own. The lord sometimes consulted his or the previous lord's wife about the choosing of names of his children or marriage partners for his family members, but he always had the final say. Once the late or contemporary lord passed away, the contemporary or new lord held a Buddhist service. While the wife of the deceased participated indirectly by sending her representative to the service, she also organized a separate Buddhist service by herself. Praying for the stability of the family and the safety of the clan was one of the practices left to these women who were not allowed to go out freely or become directly involved in politics.

In addition to these roles within the Shimazu family '*ie*' and the broader domain, the wife played an important role in the relationship between the Satsuma domain and the Tokugawa shogunate. She was in charge of gift-giving rituals (exchange of official courtesies) with the Tokugawa shogun's family. Such rituals were necessary political affairs in early modern times for the purposes of affirming the feudal master–servant relationship and maintaining political power. At the domain level, the feudal lord, his legitimate wife, and the rest of the family practiced the rituals with their vassals at annual events and family members' life-stage ceremonies to affirm and maintain their lord–vassal relationships. Regarding the rituals with the Tokugawa shogun's family, at the annual events and life-stage ceremonies of the Tokugawa family, the lord of a *daimyō* family himself or his male vassal as his envoy visited Edo castle to exchange official courtesies by greeting the shogun or his officials and delivering gifts or letters at the *omote* (official space of the shogunate). In the case of the Satsuma domain, the rituals were performed by the legitimate wife in addition to those conducted by the feudal lord. The wife sent her female vassal to Edo castle as her envoy who would be ushered into the *ōoku* (residential space of the Tokugawa family) to greet the shogun and his legitimate wife or their female vassals, deliver letters and gifts from the wife of the feudal lord, and received replies and return gifts from them. Thus, the rituals of the lord were performed by men at the *omote* while those of the wife were performed by women at the *oku* (Figure 3.1).

A survey of the families who were allowed to send female envoys to Edo castle has revealed the following information. The practice of the legitimate wife engaging in rituals with the shogun's family was limited to the branch families of the Tokugawa clan and those with relations with the Tokugawa family through marriage, such as the Shimazu family and the Date family. When was the relationship between the Shimazu family and the Tokugawa family established and what was its nature?

The marriage that established relations with the shogun's family
Kame, the daughter of the third lord of Satsuma domain, Tsunataka Shimazu, and Iehisa Konoe, a court noble, became officially engaged in 1700. This engagement came about because of a longstanding relation between the Shimazu family and the Konoe family. Iehisa was the nephew of Hiroko, the wife of the next (sixth) shogun Ienobu Tokugawa. This engagement established the Shimazu family's relation with the shogun's family through the Konoe family. After this engagement, Kame and Fuku, the wife of the fourth lord of Satsuma, Yoshitaka Shimazu, began to practice gift-giving rituals with the shogun's family at the instruction of the shogunate. Fuku became the first wife who sent a female envoy to Edo castle, and the practice of the rituals continued between the successive wives of Shimazu and the Tokugawa family. Although the engagement did not result in marriage due to Kame's death from an illness, Iehisa was

Figure 3.1: The structure of the channels through omote *and* oku

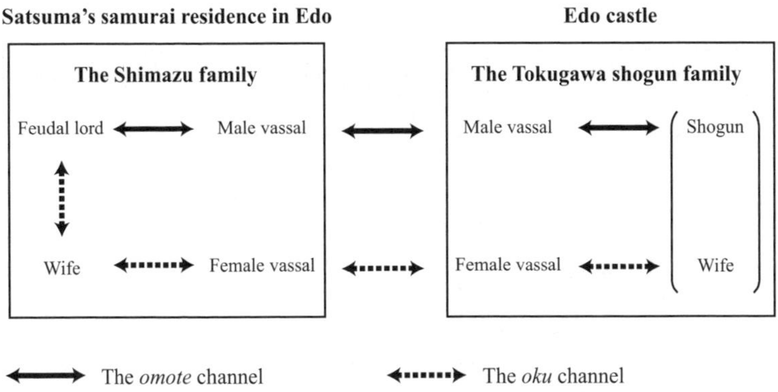

Satsuma's samurai residence in Edo		Edo castle	
The Shimazu family	⟷	**The Tokugawa shogun family**	
Feudal lord ⟷ Male vassal		Male vassal ⟷ Shogun	
⇅			
Wife ⋯⋯▶ Female vassal	◀⋯⋯▶	Female vassal ◀⋯⋯▶ Wife	

⟷ The *omote* channel   ◀⋯⋯▶ The *oku* channel

later engaged to Mitsu, the daughter of Yoshitaka, and married her in 1712 (Figure 3.2).

The Shimazu family's matrimonial union with the Konoe family, to which the wife of the shogun belonged, eventually led to further marital relations where the adopted daughter of a shogun became a Satsuma lord's legitimate wife and two of the Shimazu daughters became the legitimate wives of shoguns.[12] These events had a significant impact on the Shimazu family's relationship with the shogun's family until the end of the Edo period.

Functions of the oku *channel*
Two ritual channels were established between the feudal lord's household and the Tokugawa shogun's household: the lord's rituals were performed by men at the *omote* through the *omote* channel between the lord, his male envoy, and the shogun's family (his male vassals) and the wife's rituals were performed by women at the *oku* through the *oku* channel between the wife, her female envoy, and the shogun's family (his female vassals). Below I analyze how the *oku* channel was used in order to highlight its characteristics.

Once the *oku* channel was established, the feudal lord sometimes used the *oku* channel as well as the *omote* channel to communicate and exchange gifts or letters with the shogun's family. The party (members of the shogun's family) with whom communication and gifts or letters were exchanged through the *oku* channel and the manner of such exchanges sometimes differed from those conducted through the *omote* channel. Any inquiries regarding rituals through

Figure 3.2: The relation by marriage between the Shimazu family and the Konoe family

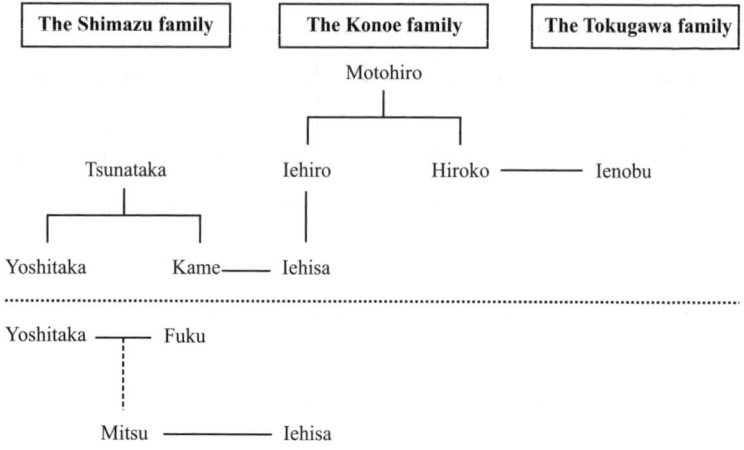

the *oku* channel were made through the *oku* channel, not the *omote* channel, to female vassals in the *ōoku* of the shogun's family who issued instructions in return. The *oku* channel was used not only by the Shimazu family but also by the shogun's family. When the Shimazu family received gifts from the shogun through the *oku* channel, they offered their gratitude to the shogun through it. Thus, the *omote* and *oku* channels were operated separately; the *omote* channel was managed by male officials of the shogunate and the *oku* channel was managed by its female vassals.

The *oku* channel was also used for purposes other than rituals. Both the Shimazu family and the shogun's family used the *oku* channel for confidential negotiations leading up to the official decision for a marriage between the shogun's adopted daughter and the feudal lord. It was also used for private discussion about the lord's retirement and the coming-of-age ceremony for the heir. In other words, confidential negotiations and private discussions about important succession matters were carried out through the *oku* channel.

I now consider the functions of the *oku* channel based on the above discussion. The Satsuma domain made a request to the shogunate at every change of lordship or shogunship for permission to use the *oku* channel for presentation by the lord or his wife according to precedent. While the rituals performed through the *omote* channel comprised public and official political affairs based on the feudal master–servant relationship between the shogunate and the Satsuma domain, the rituals through the *oku* channel were exchanged on the basis of the private relation between the Tokugawa family and the Shimazu family, and therefore the latter strived to maintain this avenue and the close relationship with the Tokugawa family. Both the Satsuma domain and the shogunate actively made use of the *oku* channel for confidential political negotiations. The following peculiarities of the *oku* space are the reasons why the *oku* channel was able to have a political function. Access to the *oku* space was stringently controlled and it was clearly separated from the *omote* space. Also, it was the area occupied by the power holder (shogun or lord), his family, and their close female vassals. Due to these factors, the Satsuma domain and the shogunate were able to convey important political information in confidence through the *oku* channel. While the feudal lord was able to use both the *omote* and *oku* channels, his wife was only able to use the *oku* channel. Nevertheless, the political function of the *oku* channel meant that the legitimate wife and female vassals of the Shimazu family and the legitimate wife and female vassals of the shogun's family fulfilled their political roles indirectly through their involvement in the *oku* channel.

The marriages of daughters and '*ie*' politics

Let us look at the daughters of a feudal lord. When his children reached adulthood, male children other than the heir were adopted by his vassals' families and became vassals of the domain while female children married into his vassals' families or other *daimyōs*' families to be their legitimate wives.

In the family of the vassal into which the lord's daughter married as the legitimate wife, sometimes the head of the family or his son was given the lord's family name or part of his first name, and sometimes the land owned by the lord's daughter/vassal's wife was passed on to her son after her death. These were special dispensations made by the feudal lord on the basis of a marital relation or at the request of the daughter he married off.

Chizuru, the elder sister of the first Satsuma lord Iehisa, suggested to him that he grant his children's lands to his vassals at the time of the redistribution of the vassals' fiefs in order to facilitate the reorganization. Iehisa took Chizuru's advice as he thought the granting of his family members' lands to his vassals would strengthen their lord–vassal relationships, extend his rule and lead to the stabilization of his domain. Shōjuin, the daughter of the ninth lord Narinobu, was raised by the Tanegashima family, a vassal, since her childhood and later married the head of the Tanegashima family. When her husband died without leaving an heir, she acted as the *de facto* head of the family by order of the Satsuma lord and supervised the management of the politics in her family's fief until a new head was put in position. She toured her family fief, planned and directed civil engineering works, and completed a three-year project. In order to avoid running down the fief's finances on such works, she paid the costs out of her privy purse as well as obtaining a subsidy from the Satsuma lord.[13]

In the Satsuma domain, the lord's wife, daughters, and concubines possessed their own lands and privy purses. Unlike the fief of the feudal lord and his male vassals based on their feudal master–servant relationships, these assets held by women were less restricted in their usage. For this reason, women's lands and privy purses were sometime used to pay for policy measures within the domain.

As mentioned above, because of their family of origin, the daughters of a feudal lord were still able to make a request or a proposal to their father even after they were married off. They exerted influence on the prestige and survival of the families into which they married and even on the management of the politics in their fiefs.

The status and roles of the concubine

Feudal lords had many concubines in addition to their officially married wife registered with the shogunate. Let us examine the status of the concubine based on their actions and treatment in the domain.

According to historical materials of the domain government, there were some occasions where a concubine who had produced an heir or many children was treated as the 'local wife' of the lord in the domain. In the absence of a legitimate wife due to death or divorce the concubine was sent up to the lord's Edo residence, and her promotion to a standing that was equal to that of the legitimate wife was announced to the vassals. As a result, she was treated as the lord's *de facto* wife in the domain. An analysis of historical materials regarding funerals of the Shimazu family[14] has found that men who were buried at the Shimazu family temple included the heads of the family (from the first to 28th lord), their sons and martyrs to their masters death, and women buried there included the legitimate wives of the lords, their daughters, the concubines whose sons later attained the lordship, and senior female vassals. The Shimazu family continued to perform ancestral rituals for generations for the lords, their sons, the lord's wives, their daughters, and the concubines whose sons later attained the lordship, mistresses, and senior vassals.

It is apparent from the above that a concubine who was virtually treated as the lord's wife and became eligible for inclusion in the Shimazu family's forebears for worship played the same role as the legitimate wife within the *ie* and the domain, such as conducting services for past lords and gift-giving rituals with vassals. However, she was not involved in the other role of the legitimate wife involving the gift-giving rituals with the shogun's family, and the feudal lord never asked the shogunate to communicate with a concubine who had been promoted to legitimate wife standing.

Thus, a concubine who produced an heir or many children was effectively treated as the lord's wife within the domain, played the role of the wife within the *ie* and domain, and was included in the Shimazu family's forebears for worship upon her death. Yet, since she was not an officially wedded wife registered with the shogunate government, she was not recognized as an official member of the Satsuma domain by the shogunate and never assumed an important role in the relations between the domain and the shogunate. In other words, the status and roles of the feudal lord's wife and concubine were different between the *ie*–domain level and the shogunate–domain level.

Women's roles and gender order in the early modern commoner class

We have seen women's roles and gender order in a ruling-class *daimyō* family. Now let us examine the commoner class using a peasant (farmer) family as an example.

Firstly, according to folklore studies,[15] in the Satsuma domain, most peasant's houses consisted of the *omote* building and the *nakae* building. The *omote* building housed space for reception and sleeping. Although its pronunciation was same as *omote* in the samurai class, it was contextually different. In the *omote* building, there were four rooms such as a drawing room, an anteroom, a small drawing room, and a storage room. The *nakae* building comprised space for daily housework such as kitchen work and farm work. In the *nakae* building, there were a dirt floor that provided room for housework and farm work, and a floored room like today's kitchen-dining room. In the peasant house, while spaces were separated based on purpose of use, there was no spatial separation of the *omote* and the *oku* spheres based on gender and public/private distinctions, unlike in the aforementioned samurai residence. This was because the *ie* of a peasant in the subordinate class had no political or public function and therefore consisted entirely of a domestic or private function.

Let us look at the roles played by members of a peasant family. Men's roles inside the home included housework such as cooking and laundry and providing support and care for their parents, and those outside the home included farming, serving the other peasant family, maintaining good relations with neighbors, and being economical and saving crops for droughts so that they could help the village and the needy. Women's roles inside the home included housework such as cooking and laundry, providing support and care for their parents and parents-in-law, and helping their husbands faithfully, and those outside the home included farming, serving the other peasant family, increasing family wealth, and helping the needy. It is obvious from the above that men and women assumed similar roles inside and outside their home.

With regard to women's status within a peasant family, there have been cases in which after the death of the father, his son offered his mother the deceased father's seat and sat himself in a lower seat. There were occasions when the new head of a family not only discharged his filial duties but also gave his aging mother a higher status than himself within the family (Sugano 1999).

In the class of commoners who had to run the household without the help of servants, women could not become the head of the family in principle as they were not allowed to participate in village politics. However, they supported their marital family with their husbands and endeavored to maintain their *ie* by assuming the same roles as their husbands in and out of their homes when their fathers and husbands became unable to act as the head of the family due to illness or death. Sugano (1999) points out that children obeyed their parents unconditionally and that the father and the mother had equal status in terms of the degree of children's obedience. My analysis has confirmed that children generally treated their father and mother equally. The roles of men and women in peasant families remained the same throughout the early modern period and the beginning of modern period (the Meiji period).

What were the conditions of marriage in the commoner class in that historical context? There have been cases in which both men and women shunned marriage or remarriage even when they received recommendations from their relatives or neighbors. The reasons for their reluctance included poverty, a desire to concentrate on supporting and caring for their family, and a desire to avoid the possibility that their parents might not like the marriage partner's attitude and behavior. In fact, there were cases in which a husband divorced his wife because she did not treat his mother well. In other words, the husband gave priority to his mother over his wife in the commoner class (Sugano 1999) and both men and women prioritized the maintenance of the existing *ie* over their marriage. The following two factors enabled this mode of marriage to exist. First, the commoner's *ie* was not a power structure unlike the samurai's, and building a bond with another family held much less value or necessity to commoner families compared with samurai families. Second, commoner families were able to maintain their *ie* without resorting to a marriage that might become an unwanted burden in some circumstances, as their *ie* was supported by the mutual aid function of their village.

Former *daimyō* families and gender order in modern times

The Shimazu family at the beginning of modern times

What changes did women's roles and gender order undergo in the context of the major political and social upheaval of the Meiji Restoration? This section will examine the continuity and shifts in the transition period from early modern to modern times.

Following the return of the domain and subjects registers to the Meiji Emperor in 1869, Tadayoshi Shimazu, the last lord of Satsuma, separated the government office building and the Shimazu residence in Kagoshima castle site. The Shimazu family home lost its political function as a result. Pre-modern officials within the castle were abolished and replaced by newly employed public officials at the government offices and housekeeping officials at the residence (Morioka 2002). The Shimazu family moved out of the castle site to another residence in 1872, separating themselves from the castle completely.

The new residence was built in 1658 as the family's villa, and was refurbished and used as the main residence of the family in Kagoshima from 1872 to 1898. The house was comprised of the *omote* space including the lord's rooms and guest rooms and the *oku* space including women's, children's, and maids' rooms. The boundary between the *omote* and the *oku* was locked every night and clearly spatially separated.

The organizational aspect of the home was as follows. The *omote* had the steward and other male housekeeping staff, servants, cooks, doctors, tradesmen, and other male employees. Tadayoshi was the then head of the family who stayed in the *omote* space to conduct official duties and business from 9 a.m. after breakfast to 3 p.m., and all his general affairs were taken care of by the male housekeeping staff including lunch service. Conversely, the family spent their days in the *oku* space together with the family head's maid, the heir's maid, other children's maids, and other female employees. The family head spent his time in the *oku* space from 3 p.m. to 9 a.m. the next morning, and his breakfast and dinner were served there by female employees. In short, the *omote* was a male domain where the head of the family carried out his public duties and business with other men. The *oku* was a space for the Shimazu family and their maids where the family members led their private lives.

With regard to the guardian of the head of the family, the family precept (family constitution) laid down in 1888 stipulated that the mother should become the guardian when an underage heir became the head of the family, or an alternative person should be selected from among relatives if the mother could not become the guardian for some reason. However, the family precept set out in 1920 provided that the guardian should be selected from among male relatives or titled members of branch families. After the death of Tadayoshi in 1897, his underage son Tadashige became head of the family. Since he was still a minor, a guardian and council of household management advisors were appointed. It is unclear how Tadashige's guardian was selected, but the guardianship was given to his uncle rather than his mother, Sumako. Why was the family precept for guardianship changed and why did Sumako not become her son's guardian?

The Shimazu family precepts were based on the noble law enacted by the central government. The 1884 version of the law allowed women to be the head of the family. However, the 1907 amendment did not recognize female family heads and limited noble family headship to a male successor. This change was the likely reason for the 1920 family precept that limited the guardianship to a male relative of the family or a branch family, even though the 1888 family precept allowed the mother to become the guardian. At the time of

Tadashige's succession, the family precept allowed the mother to become the guardian, but in reality Sumako did not take up this position. There was another reason for this. The 1884 noble law stipulated those recognized as nobility. The grandparents, parents, wife, legitimate first-born son and grandson and their wives recorded on the family head's family register were recognized as nobility, but his concubine was not recognized. The 1907 revision expanded the scope of nobility to include the widow, great-grandfather, illegitimate sons and their wives, but it still excluded the concubine. The gap in status between the wife and the concubine was greater than that between legitimate and illegitimate sons. Sumako was Tadayoshi's concubine and not his legitimate wife. In other words, the legal guardian of the head of a noble family had to be from the nobility before the question of gender arose. It is likely that Sumako could not become her son's guardian because she was a concubine, and her son's uncle was appointed as guardian instead.

Alternatively, the council of household management advisors was comprised of male relatives and some leading figures of the former Satsuma domain, while the council of relatives provided by the 1920 family precept consisted of adult male relatives and titled members of branch families. Both councils discussed important matters concerning the management of the Shimazu household. This means that decisions regarding the Shimazu family's household management issues had been made by male relatives, branch family members, and advisors since the late Meiji period, and women were kept out of direct involvement.[16]

As we have seen above, although it lost its political function in modern times, the Shimazu family continued the gender system of *omote* and *oku* that dates back to the Edo period both spatially and institutionally. When the family relocated to Tokyo in 1898 towards the end of the Meiji period, its advisors tried to transform its lifestyle into a modern one. Institutionally, a status gap between the wife and the concubine remained significant, and women's right to be involved in the household management diminished in modern times. The Shimazu family formed a joint-stock company in 1922 in order to switch its privately managed business to a corporate enterprise and completely separated its home management and business operations. This division can be regarded as another turning point, in addition to the family's relocation to Tokyo, in considering the gender system and women's roles within that household.

The construction of modern gender roles and the women of the early modern samurai family

As mentioned in an earlier section of this chapter, women of the early modern (including the Warring States period) samurai family who had impacts on their domain or *ie* were, together with filial women of the peasant family, praised highly as the leading women of their home province, and their achievements were documented and used as a supplementary reader at girls' schools in modern times. This final section will analyze the cases of early modern samurai-family women documented in the supplementary reader and consider a relationship between the construction of modern gender order and the women of the early modern samurai family.

Some of the stories in the supplementary reader unfold as follows: a wise and virtuous wife's devotion to her children's development built a foundation for the revival of her family; wise feudal lords were produced by a wife who treated a concubine's daughter as if she had been her own and raised and educated her children by herself without the help of a wet nurse; a vassal's wife (Shōjuin, mentioned earlier) took charge of political management in her family's fief in the absence of an heir; and other samurai-family women's deeds of filial piety and loyalty. It was explained that the women of Satsuma in early modern times were in a position of passivity, however they were able to attain a positive standing when they became mothers and dedicated all their efforts to their children's education. The role of women of the samurai family within their *ie* was highly valued in the arena of children's education rather than in the political arena. It was the mother's wisdom and virtues, or maternal contributions that were considered valuable rather than the wife's position on political matters. The supplementary reader further points out that these women enjoyed learning. This means that they read Confucius and other Chinese classics. It was explained that these women were able to educate their children rationally because they were not only wise by nature but also well-read and reasonable.

These views on the link between the value of maternal contributions and learning had the following political and social contexts: Japan's modern state system which did not allow women's participation in politics until the revision of the universal suffrage law in 1946; a modern girls' education system designed to produce good wives and wise mothers; the gender ideology 'men should work outside the home and women should stay home and do the housework'; and the modern interpretation of the early modern Satsuma view of home education and women,[17] where home-based education, mostly the responsibility of the mother, was for practice and social education was for training in children's education. In modern times, women were excluded from the political arena, and it was considered important that they entered a private sphere called home and played the role of mother in the home-based education of children. As for modern school education, the suggested link between the contributions of the wise mother and learning pointed to the importance of the education of women, and was associated with modern girl's schooling through changing the educational content from an early modern study of the Chinese classics to a program for producing good wives and wise mothers. In girls' school education, the achievements of early modern samurai-family women were reinterpreted as contributions made by wise mothers and used in the construction of modern gender norms and values.[18]

Conclusion

In the samurai society of early modern times, state power was held by the *ie* rather than an individual. For this reason, state power and the *ie* coexisted within the castle or residence of a *daimyō* family in the ruling class. The public nature of the existence of *ie* members based on their lineage or pedigree turned their private affairs into public matters. Since the political and household management functions were not completely separated despite the spatial and institutional distinction of the *omote* and the *oku* within the castle or residence, women's roles and marriages at the *daimyō* family took on a political element and exerted influence on the *ie* and politics. In the gift-giving rituals between the *daimyō*'s wife and the shogun's family initiated by a marriage, gender-based communication and negotiation channels were established between the *daimyō*'s household and the shogun's household corresponding to the early modern gender system based on *omote* and *oku* (Figure 3.3).

Conversely, a commoner's household only played the household management function and did not occupy the public political space of *omote*. Both women and men worked in almost equal capacities to maintain their *ie*. And the maintenance of the *ie* itself at any given time was more important than building relations with another family through marriage.

In modern times, the Shimazu family's *ie* lost its political function when state power was transferred to the Meiji government and the

Figure 3.3: The structure of the Shimazu family in early modern times

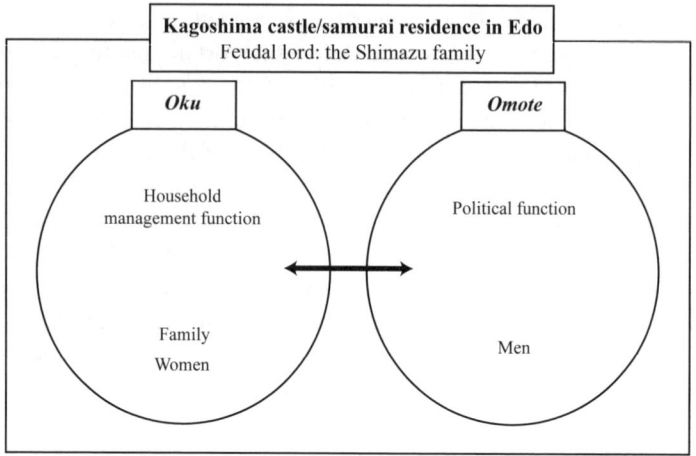

family moved out of their castle. Yet, the Shimazu residence in the Meiji period still comprised of *omote* and *oku* spheres and carried on the early modern gender system. The *omote* became the space for private business functions instead of political functions and coexisted with the *oku* space retaining a home management function. After the formation of a joint-stock company in 1922, the workplace moved out of the Shimazu family's house, resulting in a complete spatial separation of home and workplace or a complete separation of the home management function and the business function, leaving only the former in the house (Figures 3.4 and 3.5). In both early modern and modern times, emphasis was on lineage or pedigree at the Shimazu family. That brought differences in status and roles between wife and concubine.

The former *daimyō*'s *ie* lost its political function, women in modern times were barred from participation in the new regime of modern politics, and their right to be involved in household management diminished. Then women were confined within the private sphere of the home. Consequently, a new gender system and women's roles were created within the family based on the ideology of 'men should work outside the home and women should stay home and do the housework,' and greater emphasis was placed on the importance of the mother's role in children's education at home. In school education,

Figure 3.4: The structure of the Shimazu family in the Meiji period

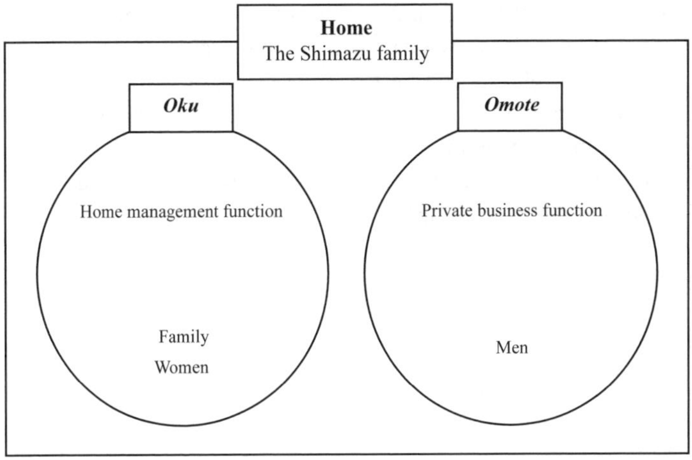

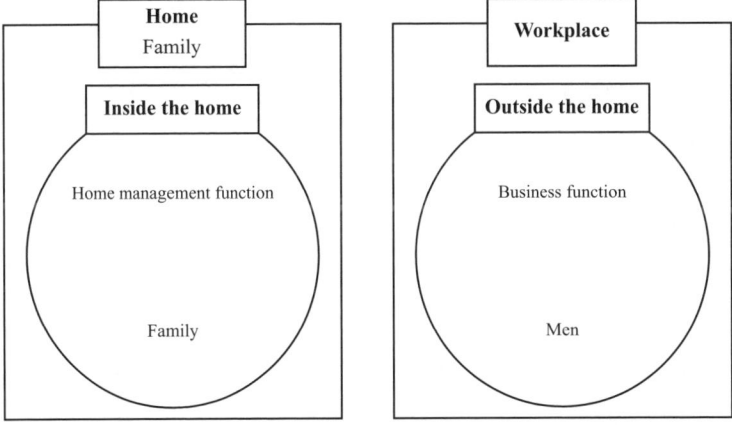

Figure 3.5: The structure of the Shimazu family in the Taishō period

the achievements of the women of early modern samurai families were recast into discourses of 'motherhood' and used in the production of 'good wives and wise mothers' and the construction of modern gender norms and values.

This chapter has presented a case study of the Satsuma domain alone. However, the findings regarding the link between the process of home–workplace separation and the changes in the gender system and women's roles within the family over the period from pre-modern times to the present can, to a certain degree, be generalized to Japanese society as a whole. Further studies must be carried out to illuminate the relationship between the states of being in the home and workplace and the changes in the gender system and women's roles at home and in society more clearly by conducting further analyses of the actual conditions as well as the institutional aspects in modern and present times.

4 Diversifying Korean Populations in Japan and a New Type of Ethnic Movement

Hyun Sun Lee

Introduction

In Japan, there exist various internally heterogeneous ethnic minority groups. Of these, the Korean community in Japan is one of the most diverse considering its history and politically aligned sectors—Chongryun and Mindan—mirroring its homelands, North and South Korea. This diasporic Korean community has become even more diverse over the period of its long residence in Japan. Concerning minorities, the issue of internal diversity tends to be overlooked or even easily ignored by treating each as a homogeneous group. However, understanding the heterogeneity of a minority group helps us to paint a proper picture of each community and to avoid further creating totalizing misrepresentations.

The Korean population in Japan has experienced a significant demographic shift in recent decades. Previous generations of Korean immigrants who migrated to Japan during the 1920s and 30s were the dominant and leading community group until the 1970s. Since the 1980s, however, the younger generations who were born and bred in Japan became dominant. While Chongryun and Mindan shared the hegemony over the Korean community of older generations, younger generations have been involved in more dynamic discourses concerning notions of community and ethnic movements. Since the late 1980s, the influence of younger generations in *zainichi*[1] activism has grown alongside the declining hegemony of traditional large organizations such as Chongryun and Mindan; many individuals have gone to the extent of leaving the community and choosing to be assimilated into Japanese society. Additionally, in a recent decade, a growing number of small and informal groups were organized targeting further integration into Japanese society (Neary 2002; Ryang 1997; Tai 2006). As we have seen, parallel to the demographic changes of the Korean population in Japan, the community witnessed the emergence of diverse ethnic identities and a reorientation of ethnic movements.

In light of the above changing circumstances of the Korean community, this study focuses specifically on the Chongryun community, affiliated with North Korea. Chongryun has played an important role in constructing and promoting the discourse inside the *zainichi* community and has maintained a separatist stance towards Japanese society and strong connections with North Korea. However, this Chongryun community is also diversifying and changing, and to examine how this has occurred and the direction in which it is heading is the main purpose of this chapter. That is, this chapter examines current challenges to the classical ethnic movement style of Chongryun in addition to emergent discourses inside the Chongryun community. Also, it investigates how some Chongryun elites reacted toward the challenges through a case study. Through presenting my case study of an ethnic movement group—Aera with Chongryun background—based on ethnographic research, I examine how this group is mobilized and how some groups of Chongryun ethnic elites have found a new way to overcome the situation of the demise in ethnic community ties.

This chapter is constructed as follows. First, to elaborate the background of the recent change in the Chongryun community, I review Chongryun's close relationship with the North Korean regime and look at how this relationship has influenced the lives of the members of the community. It is important to understand this part of the story because the relationship between Chongryun and North Korea is significant in terms of explaining recent challenges and problems raised inside the community. Second, I present the issues faced by Chongryun, positioned as the factors related to its existential crisis, and examine the socio-political backgrounds of these problems. Third, I look at Chongryun's attempt to solve its problems by reforming its organization and undergoing reorientation. Here I investigate the opinions of the *zainichi* public regarding the results of the reform. Finally, through presenting a case study of an ethnic non-profit welfare organization—Aera—I examine the emergence of the new type of ethnic movement in the *zainichi* community.

Chongryun and North Korea: an organic relationship

In October 1945, following the end of the Second World War and the emancipation of the Korean peninsular from Japan's occupation, leftist

Koreans in Japan established an ethnic organization named Choryun (the League of Koreans). Choryun was allied with the Japanese communist party and publicly showed its radically left stance. Provoked and threatened by the stance of Choryun, the Occupation Forces in Japan and Japanese authorities dissolved it without any warning in 1949. Since then intense political conflict and the rise and fall of several other ethnic organizations have occurred within the Korean community. In 1955 Chongryun was founded as part of this cycle of upheaval. While Chongryun shared many common aspects with Choryun, the former took a different political line than that of the latter. That is, while pledging its independence from the Japanese communist party, Chongryun emphasized its North Korean allegiance by defining itself as an exclusive organization of North Korean overseas nationals (Jin 2001; Lee and De Vos 1981; Ryang 1997).

Chongryun has been described as an organic corporation of North Korea, and the tight relationship between the two has been maintained through close political and financial engagement. The first distinctive aspect that is evidence of the relationship is that Chongryun's leading members have relied on North Korea's guiding principle. Chongryun's senior executives are entitled to join the governmental institution in North Korea, the 'Supreme Council of the People's Commissar' (*Chaego Inmin Whaewee*), an honor not afforded in the relationship between Mindan and the South Korean regime. Further, Chongryun's leading members have taken the matter of *Chuche* (Self-Reliance or Self-Dependence) ideology seriously, the official ideology supporting the North Korean regime. Since the 1980s, Chongryun has put more weight on establishing loyalty toward Kim Jung-il, the son and successor of Kim Il-sung, than on the ideology itself (Jin 1996: 406).

The second factor in this equation is, since the 1950s, North Korea has provided financial support to the Korean community in Japan in the form of an Educational Aid Fund. From April 1957, North Korea remitted to Chongryun through the Educational Aid Fund over 130 times, the total of which amounts to over 43 billion yen. Since the 1980s, economic hardship in North Korea has caused a significant reduction in the amount of the fund, but the funds sent to the Chongryun community were very substantial during the 1960s and 70s (Jin 2001; Lee 1981; Lee 1999a).

The Educational Aid Fund has been very influential in maintaining a tight relationship between North Korea and the Chongryun community in two ways. First, it played a major financial role in the

Chongryun Korean school system. Deprived of any financial subsidy from the Japanese state, Chongryun schools have been highly reliant on financial help from North Korea, and until the 1980s, the Educational Aid Fund 'comprised more than fifty percent of the total budget needed to carry out ethnic education' in Japan (Lee 1981: 170). Second, the fund provided the Korean community in Japan with psychological intimacy with the North Korean regime. The financial support from their 'homeland' designed to help them to maintain Korean national language and history was impressive enough for the *zainichi* community, especially in the 1950s and 60s when the majority were disadvantaged and facing social discrimination in Japan, to feel grateful for the connection with their homeland, North Korea (Jin 1996). Therefore, when the internal hegemonic map and orientation of Chongryun were set, this sentiment was important in that it provided legitimacy and hegemony to the group supporting exclusive allegiance with the North Korean regime, severing any ties with the Japanese Communist Party (Jin 1996). Even to this time, from the perspective of a quarter of the Chongryun community, this financial help has been regarded as a great debt of gratitude to their homeland of North Korea, and the ethnic schools as the results of the fund have been a core institution maintaining the connection between North Korea and Chongryun.

Third, since the 1970s the above flow of remittance has reversed its trend, that is, the money began to flow from Chongryun to North Korea. This was conducted in two major forms: remittance from Chongryun to North Korea, and through 'joint enterprises between North Korea and the merchants and industrialists of the Chongryun community' (Jin 1996: 24). Starting in the early 1970s remittance has systematically been directed to North Korea, and from this point the amount of remittance from Chongryun to Korea exceeded that flowing in the other direction. North Korea named these two processes a 'Patriotic Cause' (*Aegook Saup, Aikoku jigyō*) and has required continuous economic support from Chongryun (Jin 1996; Lee 1999a, 1999b). Through these political and financial interactions, Chongryun and North Korea have maintained particularly close relations.

Signs of crisis in Chongryun

Since the 1980s, some of the problems faced by Chongryun began to float to the surface, and particularly in recent decades, these problems were identified as a sign of Chongryun's existential crisis. The first issue is that Chongryun's affiliates have continuously seceded. Though the official membership of Chongryun is never publicized, a few factors have been internally used to estimate the decrease in membership such as the number of subscriptions to the organizational bulletin, *Chosun Shinbo*, the number of students enrolled in Chongryun schools, and the number of changes of nationality from *Chosun* to South Korean (Jin 2001; Chung 2005). Especially considering the symbolic meaning of ethnic education in the community, the shrinking number of ethnic school children is the most vivid phenomenon in revealing the decline of the Chongryun community. Even though the Japanese educational system has provided the major education institutions for the majority of *zainichi* children, the ethnic school has been highly appreciated by *zainichi* people, especially by those closely affiliated with Chongryun. However, the number of Chongryun school students and that of Chongryun schools have significantly decreased for the last decade.

The second problem Chongryun faces is the current financial hardship of their organization. Japanese economic stagnation in the 1990s made a serious impact on the *zainichi* business sector, and particularly, it caused the collapse of many branches of the Credit Association of Chosun Bank (Chogin Shinyōkumiai), the so-called 'Chogin.' The Chogin was the centre of the *zainichi* economy with 36 unions and 176 branches, and became insolvent when a large number of *zainichi* companies went bankrupt during the Japanese economic stagnation. Chogin's collapse had a significant impact on the *zainichi* economy. This was understood as an event that signified Chongryun's poor business management in the financial sector (Lee 2004; Jin 1996).

Due to the deteriorated financial situation of Chongryun, a large amount of Chongryun's common assets were taken as security by Japanese banks. Further, this caused the problem of insufficient or even delayed salary payment to the approximately 8,500 staff members of Chongryun. In light of this situation, many staff members could not afford to maintain their lifestyles, and a growing number of them had to leave their jobs (Lee 2000: 36). This financial pressure also affected the Chongryun schools. The decreasing number of students, reduced educational funds from North Korea, and reduced donations from businesspeople in the Chongryun community resulted in reduced or unpaid salaries for the teachers.

Increasing social antagonism against the North Korean regime and Chongryun

The aforementioned problems Chongryun has faced can be summarized as seceding affiliates and financial hardships. These problems have been created and exacerbated in recent decades due to a few socio-political reasons. At the centre of these reasons were the aforementioned long-standing relationship between North Korea and Chongryun and demographical and ideological changes in the rank and file of the Chongryun community. In this section, these socio-political factors causing the current problems and crisis of Chongryun will be investigated.

The first background factor in Chongryun's crisis was the deteriorated state of relations between Japan and North Korea and the diminishing state power of the latter (Chung 2005). As mentioned above, Chongryun has identified itself as an organization of overseas North Korean nationals and has maintained organic and close relations with North Korea. Therefore, the images of North Korea and international relations between North Korea and Japan have inevitably influenced the lives of *zainichi* populations. However, through various events and issues over time, a negative perception of North Korea has grown in both the *zainichi* community and the Japanese society more broadly.

Until the 1980s, several issues related to North Korea had left the *zainichi* community disappointed with both Chongryun and North Korea. These representative events boil down to the 'Movement for Repatriation to North Korea' (*Booksong Saup*) through the 1960s,[2] several large terrorist attacks on South Korea, and the patrimonial transmission of power in the North Korean regime (Jin 1996; Lee 1999a). These issues eventually caused a negative stance against North Korea inside the *zainichi* community and promoted secession from Chongryun.

If the above issues contributed to a negative perspective of Chongryun and North Korea inside the *zainichi* community rather than in the Japanese society more broadly, several issues raised since the 1990s caused a negative perception of North Korea and Chongryun from both the *zainichi* community and the Japanese society. Since the mid-90s North Korea has initiated several military actions such as the 1994 development of nuclear power and the 1998 missile-test. Japanese mass media widely covered and strongly criticized North Korea's threatening poses, emphasizing all other negative aspects of North

Korea. This fostered hostile public opinion in the Japanese society towards North Korea, and the Chongryun community directly related to North Korea also became a target of social hostility. This situation became decisively worse after the so-called shock of '9.17'; that is, Kim Jung-il's admission of abduction of Japanese citizens by North Korea in his meeting with the then-Japanese Prime Minister Koizumi visiting Pyongyang on September 17, 2002.

The abduction issue was more influential than any other previous issue in constructing antagonistic public opinions among the Japanese toward North Korea and Chongryun, and the Chongryun community became isolated in the Japanese society (McCormack and Haruki 2005). Whenever relations between Japan and North Korea worsened and the Japanese social mood became antagonistic towards North Korea, Chongryun has provided an alternative target of offensive and criminal behaviors founded on hostility against North Korea; for example, Chongryun schools and offices received threats of bombing attacks, and there were several incidences of harassment of Chongryun school children on their way to school. However, this time in addition to such offences from a sector of the Japanese public, Japanese police and the government also joined in and frequently conducted 'very politically motivated' monitoring and investigation of the *zainichi* community (Takahashi 2007: para. 6). According to Takahashi, 'there has been a tendency to consider everything related to the North, whether directly or indirectly, as a form of evil' since 9.17, and Japanese police and government authorities became more active in conducting arrests and house searches targeting the Chongryun community (2007: para. 4). Under the circumstances, Chongryun lost a large part of its support from both the *zainichi* community and the Japanese society since 9.17, serving to worsen the isolation of Chongryun. Many Japanese and *zainichi* groups of former pro-Pyongyang and pro-Chongryun sentiment were disappointed with North Korea and Chongryun and at the same time, they could no longer maintain their stance for fear of the social disadvantages coming from the mood of hostility in general (Hong 2004).[3]

Orientation of Chongryun and growing community demands

The largest and most important reason causing the secession from Chongryun within the *zainichi* community is Chongryun's maladjustment to the changing and growing social demands inside the community. For the new generations of *zainichi* who were born and grew up in Japan, repatriation to Korea is not realistic at all, and the politics of their homelands is somewhat a matter too removed from their everyday lives. This does not mean that they are searching only for assimilation into the Japanese society; for some, matters of ethnicity, ethnic identity, and ethnic community are still meaningful enough to various degrees. However, they want an ethnic organization like Chongryun to play an effective role in improving the lives of the *zainichi* population. That is, they expect the organization to focus on enhancing the civil rights and welfare of the *zainichi* while helping them to maintain their ethnic identity. However, Chongryun did not abandon their politically oriented activities in relation to North Korea and has continued to emphasize the matter of ideology and support for the Kim Jung-il regime.

This dissonance in orientation has been most frequently and seriously raised in the area of ethnic education. As mentioned above, in the *zainichi* community ethnic education since starting in the 1950s has been eroded, but is still regarded as a symbol of ethnic identity and the core of the ethnic community. In actuality, the majority of *zainichi* children have attended Japanese schools rather than ethnic schools since the 1970s (Chung 2005; Rohlen 1981); further, the number of students has steadily declined in recent decades. As one of the reasons for such a decline, the ideology-based education of Chongryun schools was identified, and calls were made for the reform of the curriculum and the entire operating style of ethnic schools. As a result, in the 1993–95 revision of the Chongryun school curriculum, such requests were somewhat accepted by reducing ideological contents and adding more subject matter about the Japanese society (Ryang 1997: 51–67). However, this did not satisfy the public, and in 1998 another objection occurred over the matter of the school curriculum, known as '*Yomangsuh sakun*' (the matter of a written request).[4] This revealed the ongoing conflict between Chongryun and *zainichi* community members over the issue of the orientation of Chongryun. This unprecedented collective action caused large controversy in the Chongryun community (Lee 1999a).

Chongryun's trial for reorientation and an unsatisfied *zainichi* public

In light of the sign's of Chongryun's crisis, the organization could not continue to ignore the voices of criticism against its orientation and operation. In 1999, Chongryun's leading members took a gesture towards reforming Chongryun to tackle all the problems it was facing and to adapt itself to the new social demands. On September 21, 1999, Chongryun officially presented its reorientation at the Third Session of the 18th Expanded Convention of the Central Committee of Chongryun (*Chosun Shinbo*, September 27, 1999). This was interpreted as Chongryun's intention to change from an ideology-oriented organization to an ethnic one for the sake of community members in terms of their civil rights, economic interests, and welfare (Jin 2001),[5] through focusing on the wellbeing of the *zainichi* public while distancing itself from the North Korean regime. This manifestation of the reform and reorientation was largely welcomed in the Chongryun community with the expectation of the implementation of proper countermeasures to Chongryun's crisis.

However, a few years later the community saw a series of internal resistance events revealing that Chongryun's attempt of 1999 was not entirely successful. Some events occurring in the 2000s revealed that Chongryun's reforms did not work in practice and rather escalated the grievances of the community's rank and file about Chongryun. The stance of Chongryun toward the aforementioned 9.17 event, i.e. Kim Jung-il's admission of abducting Japanese citizens, was one important point revealing the internal conflicts caused by the community's disappointment with Chongryun's leading members. Chongryun, having denied the matter of abduction to both the Japanese and the *zainichi* public until 9.17, did not mention it or make any apology even after it turned out to be true (Huh 2003). This provoked many community members and caused several local-level acts of resistance against the orientation of the central administration in the form of independent action such as public apologies about the abduction to the Japanese society. The central administration of Chongryun, however, seriously criticized such independent actions (*Hankyuhrae* June 1, 2005).

The event that revealed in a more direct way the inadequacies of Chongryun's reform occurred a few years later. In September 2004, a sensational long essay was loaded on Chongryun's webpage entitled 'A Suggestion for the Reform and Revival of Chongryun in the Twenty-first Century.' This essay criticized the Chongryun organization as undemocratic and rigid and predicted its extinction in the future unless critical reforms were undertaken. It argued that despite the ongoing requirement of changes from the community, Chongryun has adhered to the old practices and been obsessed with its strong relationship with North Korea even in the 2000s. It also pointed out that Chongryun's reform trial of 1999 has never been put into practice and argued that there has never been a real intention to undertake the reforms. It criticized the top-down management structure of Chongryun that ignored the voices of local people at a grassroots level. While the author of the essay, Hong Kyung-ee, an incumbent Chongryun officer, was alleged by Chongryun through *Chosun Shinbo* (Chongryun's bulletin) to be a spy from South Korea supported by the Japanese government, many Chongryun workers at the branch-level expressed their support for Hong's opinions (*Hankyuhrae* June 1, 2005).[6]

Most of the critical voices, including the aforementioned incidents of 'rebellion,' share a common understanding of Chongryun's situation: Chongryun has not changed at all even after the declaration of organizational reform. That is, they pointed out that while the rank and file of the community is changing ideologically and demographically, the Chongryun organization has been lagging behind and has not properly adapted to the situation. In other words, while the *zainichi* people started to expect the Chongryun organization to play a more practical role as an ethnic organization, Chongryun has adhered to its old role as a dispatched organization of North Korea and still emphasizes the rivalry with South Korean-affiliated Mindan. The conservative and undemocratic operation style of the organization disabled the implementation of reform, and the critical voices and suggestions from the grassroots level were not accepted and simply ignored. This leads Chongryun's critics to the conclusion: if this situation is maintained, Chongryun cannot be guaranteed of its future existence.

The emergence of a new type of ethnic movement in the Chongryun community

The aforementioned acts of rebellion occurring inside the Chongryun community could be understood as mere occasional events if they were resolved and not followed by any further community actions. However, through examining a case study of a small group—Aera organization—it is found that the understanding that the existence of Chongryun and the ethnic community itself is in danger did not manifest simply through critical voices, but played a role in mobilizing a sector of ethnic elites to break away from Chongryun and form a new group to conduct its own style of ethnic movement. By introducing their activities and voices, I hope to suggest the diversification of Chongryun's elite group. In mobilizing this group, the influence of the changed social circumstances such as state policy changes resulting in the expansion of resources available to ethnic groups is also critically important. However, in this chapter I hope to limit the focus to the influence of more socio-psychological factors in the mobilization of ethnic movements.

The demographic situation of the *zainichi* population with rapid ageing and the privatization of social welfare services through the introduction of the Long-term Care Insurance (*Kaigo Hoken*) system by the Japanese state gave momentum to certain *zainichi* groups to be proactive. From the late 1990s and early 2000s, day-care facilities for elderly *zainichi* began to be opened by a few *zainichi* groups centering on the Kansai area. By 2004, the number of institutions providing similar services amounted to over 36 in the Kansai area. Among them, Aera was one of the pioneering and successful groups founded in K city in November 1999 to provide the *zainichi* community with social welfare services, especially care services for older members of the community.

The legal status of Aera is defined as a non-profit organization and a long-term care service provider dedicated by the Japanese government. Also, its ethnic background as a group of Koreans could be identified from its official title. However, it was evident that Aera intended to not mention or actively identify its relationship with Chongryun. Rather, they emphasized that the group and its facilities took a neutral position in terms of its affiliation or relationship with the large organizations like Chongryun and Mindan. However, through my interviews and observations, I established that Aera is largely reliant on its Chongryun community background.

Aera's Chongryun background is initially evident from the profile of its staff members. Most staff members were educated in Chongryun ethnic schools; and especially the administrative staff were graduates of Chosun University, a Chongryun-affiliated university in Japan, and many were previously employed at Chongryun-affiliated institutions such as Chongryun schools, the Chongryun newspaper company, and Chongryun-branch offices etc. They told me that they had hardly ever before had a chance to work for or with the Japanese; and that they did not want to do either. Therefore, a dominant aspect of the social networks and capital of the members was based on the Chongryun community. Secondly, active interrelations with other Chongryun institutions were another sign of Aera's relationship with Chongryun. During my fieldwork, Aera sought cooperation from Chongryun-affiliated groups in organizing various events and a close relationship with those groups was maintained to a substantial level in conducting its activities.

Considering only the profile of staff members and its maintained relationship with Chongryun affiliates, Aera may be viewed as another subsidiary of Chongryun. However, Aera has several aspects distinctive from the traditional large ethnic organizations like Chongryun and Mindan and their activities. First, as opposed to the Chongryun organization the focus of Aera's activities was not aimed towards the political matters of the homeland, but towards the provision of social welfare services to meet the practical needs of the *zainichi* public. Second, Aera obtained the independent legal status of a non-profit organization rather than remaining as a part of Chongryun as an umbrella organization. Third, as the above aspects imply, Aera is actively involved with the Japanese society. Since its formation, Chongryun has maintained its stance separating the community from the Japanese society. This stance was based on Chongryun's political allegiance to North Korea with principles of non-interference with the Japanese state and its policies and on its fear of assimilation through frequent and profound contact with the Japanese society. However, in the case of Aera, it modified Chongryun's long-sustained separatist stance and started to be actively involved with the Japanese society by participating in the Japanese welfare system and civil society.

Aera's movement separating itself from the activities and system of the Chongryun organization and actively using the Japanese system may be understood to imply that it is simply striving for the inclusion of *zainichi* into Japanese society. However, its motivations and the details of its activities share many aspects with the ethos of the existing Chongryun movement. Aera shares with Chongryun a strong anti-assimilation stance and emphasizes the preservation of Korean ethnicity. And, the preservation of a robust Korean ethnic community and ethnicity is Aera's major goal. Therefore, in conducting its activities and promoting its integration into Japanese society, Aera did not sacrifice ethnicity; rather, it strongly emphasized the issue of ethnicity throughout its activities. The most distinctive and representative element revealing this aspect is a style of care service that Aera promotes: *Woori-shiki Kaigo* (Our mode of care). Aera named its own care-service style *Woori-shiki Kaigo* that they argue was designed specifically for the *zainichi* elderly. Simply put, *Woori-shiki Kaigo* emphasizes the importance of introducing attributes of ethnicity in care services. Aera argues that the Japanese welfare system, including social care for the aged, has been designed and implemented for the 'Japanese' only ignoring the existence of members of different ethnic groups. It insists that because of this aspect of Japanese social welfare services, *zainichi* elderly cannot fully use the system. By introducing ethnic elements into care services such as Korean language, pastime culture, foods, staff members, and co-users, Aera emphasizes the importance of preserving ethnic cultures and ethos. In other words, Aera understands its activities as the ethnic movement that is working to preserve Korean ethnicity among the *zainichi* populations.

Then, why were Aera members mobilized to take different strategies to that of Chongryun as presented above, even though they shared with Chongryun the idea that the preservation of ethnicity is an ultimate value for them? Through my ethnography, I found that Aera understands that to achieve its goal of preserving the 'Koreanness' and Korean community it needs to stop the secession of community members by providing what the rank and file of the community want. However, as we reviewed earlier, Chongryun has not proven itself to be overly effective in doing the work. Those who established and developed Aera regard the situation as threatening to the existence of the community. Aera members understood that if they do not do something to meet the emergent needs of community members, they would leave the community to be actively involved with the Japanese system without any choice. Aera also feels that such situation will finally lead to the demise of the ethnic community and the gradual assimilation into Japanese society. Therefore, they established a welfare organization to meet high social demands to attract people to the ethnic community. They think that providing particularly the elderly care services, which the entire society has high demand for due to a rapidly ageing society, would satisfy both older and younger generations and make them feel more intimate with and grateful towards ethnic activism and organizations.

Also, the fact that Aera was adopting the independent status of NPO rather than being part of Chongryun organization was advantageous to Aera. First, Aera could gain broader and more active support from both the *zainichi* community and the Japanese society. According to interviews and internal documents, these days inside the *zainichi* community, many *zainichi* want a robust ethnic community and the preservation of ethnicity but do not want to support Chongryun. For example, many people who willingly donate to ethnic schools with the expectation that it can really contribute to the preservation of ethnicity refuse to donate to Chongryun itself as they have lost faith in the organization. This trend is especially strong among *zainichi* from the business sector, because for a long time they suffered from exploitation from Chongryun to support North Korea in the name of 'Patriotic Cause.' However, Aera with independent status could mobilize such people from both the *zainichi* community and Japanese society who hope to contribute to the ethnic community but are reluctant at being involved with Chongryun as supporters or even staff members.

Not only separating itself from Chongryun, but also acquiring the Non-profit Organization legal status with its board of directors including people from outside Chongryun such as Japanese intellectuals and Mindan-affiliated figures, Aera could be accepted as a part of Japanese civil society. This was particularly helpful for Japanese and *zainichi* sympathetic to *zainichi* activism including Chongryun but having felt pressure not to participate due to hostile social moods against Chongryun and North Korea. This also was welcomed by *zainichi* supporters fed up with political rivalry between Chongryun and Mindan and desirous of a neutral form of ethnic movement group that they can support on a more casual level. The NPO status enabled Aera to be more easily connected to the image and rhetoric of volunteerism and multicultural coexistence and helped both *zainichi* and Japanese supporters to join with much less concern. Actually, Aera has gained a large amount of donations from both *zainichi* and Japanese that has significantly contributed to its activities and constructing facilities.

Conclusion

Since its establishment, Chongryun has identified itself as an organization directly affiliated with North Korea and maintained tight relations with that state. Until the late 1970s, it shared hegemony over the *zainichi* population with Mindan, and has led the discourses on the *zainichi* community and ethnicity with strong organizational power and broad support from both the *zainichi* public and many Japanese intellectuals. Also, based on its non-interference principle with Japanese policies and politics, the guiding principles of North Korea, and its strong reluctance to assimilate to the Japanese society, Chongryun has maintained its separatist stance in Japan.

However, since the 1980s Chongryun has started to face several problems, and the situation has deteriorated since. In the 1990s and 2000s it was understood that Chongryun is even facing an existential crisis. Chongryun's biggest problems are the facts that it is continuously losing its affiliates over time and that it suffers serious financial hardships. These problems were caused by several sociopolitical reasons such as growing social hostility toward North Korea and Chongryun and Chongryun's lagging behind the increasing social demands of the ethnic community. That is, the antagonistic social moods increased the number of people who stopped supporting Chongryun from both the *zainichi* community and Japanese society. Further, those whose practical needs were not satisfied by Chongryun focusing on only the politics of North Korea and political rivalry with Mindan also left the community.

Coming from various internal conflicts and criticisms of the Chongryun community, in the late 1990s Chongryun took action to change its orientation and reform its organization by suggesting changes from a politics-based organization to one for the welfare and civil rights of community members. However, it so happened that these gestures made by Chongryun did not take any practical form, and Chongryun has repeated its old adamant operating style even after the manifestation of reform. This disappointed the rank and file of Chongryun, and the aforementioned problems of Chongryun have become even more serious.

The disappointment with Chongryun and the fear for the extinction of the ethnic community mobilized some Chongryun elites to break away from Chongryun and establish their own ethnic organization for community revival. The Aera group is a good example of such movement. Based on their aim of ethnic resilience, Aera shared the idea with Chongryun that assimilation of the *zainichi* public to the Japanese society should be avoided, and that preserving ethnicity and maintaining a robust ethnic community is essential. However, Aera did not maintain Chongryun's style but conducted its activities and formed its strategy in its own way. That is, it did not maintain Chongryun's separatist stance, but actively joined the Japanese system and civil society for its own purpose. Rather than focusing on the politics of the homelands as Chongryun has done, Aera directed its activities toward the provision of social welfare services to the ethnic community, especially aged care services in high demand by the entire society. Also, by separating itself from Chongryun and participating in the Japanese civil society through attaining NPO legal status, it was able to attract a much larger support-base from both the *zainichi* community and Japanese society, people who have felt reluctant to become involved with Chongryun. Also, their legal status could assist Aera to take full advantage of all the discourses and rhetoric of Japanese society. The emergence of this new type of ethnic movement implies a more diversifying Chongryun community and this may be evidence that future Chongryun community members and elites can take new directions to adapt to the new circumstances of the ethnic community.

5 Dealing with the Past: The Construction of Subjectivity in the Japanese American Reparation Movement

Kumiko Tsuchida

Introduction

This chapter analyses the life histories of the activists who partially but significantly led the Japanese American redress movement that occurred from the 1970s through the 1990s in the United States. The aim of their movement was to pursue reparations for the tangible and intangible losses inflicted on the Japanese immigrants and their descendants during the Second World War.[1] Approximately 110,000 Japanese Americans were forcefully relocated to the internment camps by the US government, immediately after Japan's Pearl Harbor attack in 1941.[2]

The Japanese American reparation movement was certainly a case where an echo from the past catches the attention in a different sociohistorical context. A few decades after the events in question actually occurred, the movement challenged the legitimacy of the internment policy to US society and the Japanese American community itself. Some of the actual internment victims had already passed away and the rest were aging when the idea of claiming reparation was proposed to the Japanese American community in the 1970s. Although an actual victim who was interned when he was a teenager first put the claim forward, it did not fully achieve the support of other victims. Rather, particularly in the initial stages of the movement, support for the reparation proposal came from the younger generation who had no memory or experience of internment (Takezawa 1994; Murray 1995). Why did this happen? Why did these members of the younger generation participate in claiming reparation despite the fact that they did not remember or experience wartime internment? And how did they speak of the wartime internment in the context of the 1970s?

Dealing with the past

The Japanese American movement is located in a global trend of reparation movements (Yamamoto 1999 and 2001; Brooks 1999;

Torpey 2003).³ Although reparation claims over past injustices are not a modern phenomenon, those that occurred in the recent past were probably expedited by the reparation of Holocaust survivors in the post-Second World War era. Since then, we have seen a great number of reparation claims over perceived injustices on a global scale, whatever the form the reparation takes (Brooks 1999). The examples of this phenomenon are too many to enumerate. In terms of reparation claims, people in post-colonial countries such as New Zealand have blamed the old oppressors for exploitative treatment. Some of the victimized groups have denounced the respective foreign government for war crimes, as has occurred in China and Korea for example. In other cases, minority groups reveal the disenfranchising and discriminatory policies of their own government, such as in the US and Australia. While the origin of claims are diverse, claims for reparation make us face the past which remains unhealed and often leads us to search for ways to 'come to terms with the past' (Cairns 2003).

The frequent occurrence of reparation claims and their implementation have stimulated much controversy. First, a reparation claim, especially when it is socially acknowledged, could entail rewriting or amending history. This is a possibility as the reparation publically exposes the injustices of past treatment either unknown or justified in some way until the claim surfaces. Second, the reparation trend draws attention to the contents and forms of reparation (Brooks 2003). The substance and types of reparation vary case by case, regardless of the scale of damage. Some groups receive monetary compensation or some form of material reparation, but others achieve merely an apology or acknowledgement. In most reparation cases, however, it is impossible to completely regain what had once been destroyed or seized. Claimants, therefore, gain symbolic meaning to varying degrees from the process of reparation. Torpey points to the fact that one of the contemporary features of reparation claims is that more attention is paid to 'psychic harms' than before (2003: 4). The symbolic meaning drawn from some forms of reparation and indeed the *process* of demanding and obtaining reparation could thus be seen as healing to some extent for the victims, as in the case of the survivors of the Japanese American internment policy.

Third, the increasing number of reparation claims raises the issue of the effectiveness of the movements. In this regard, the Japanese American reparation movement has provided a model to successfully redress claims. Their movement achieved public apology and monetary compensation under the enactment of the Civil Liberties Act of 1988. Drawing ideas empirically and theoretically from the example of the Japanese American movement, studies on reparation movements examine valid approaches for achieving successful reparation claims (Howard-Hassmann 2004; Brooks 2003). One of the studies suggests that among the key elements for reparation movements, it is important to frame the damages of the past in a form applicable to the present context, and to make this narrative resonate with the others in order to mobilize diverse forms of support (Howard-Hassman 2004: 824, 827). However, these discussions fail to consider subjectivity to a sufficient extent in the context of reparation movements. That is, who is to be a subject to speak of the past damages and move the redress claim forward in the present? This problem is more crucial when the perceived harm occurred generations ago or when many, but not all, of the actual victims have already passed away at the time of the claim.

The Japanese American movement is suggestive when considering notions of subjectivity in the context of reparation movements. Through a case study of the Japanese American reparation movement, this chapter examines how an individual could be a subject of the reparation movement when he/she is not an actual victim of the perceived harms. For this purpose, this chapter elucidates the life histories of younger generation activists involved in the movement. In this regard, I focus on members of the National Coalition for Redress/Reparations (NCRR). NCRR was one of the three main organizations that led the Japanese American reparation movement. Unlike the other two organizations (the Japanese American Citizens League and the National Council for Japanese American Redress), however, NCRR was primarily formed by members of the younger second and third generation of the Japanese immigrants who had a dim memory of the internment as they were infants at the time or did not experience the internment.[4]

From 2004 until 2008, I collected ethnographic data from the founding members of the NCRR. Among six of the founding members whom I interviewed, I focus on Mary Kimoto, a third generation Japanese American who was born after the Second World War. Her life history shows commonality with the other members in many ways, but more importantly, it indicates most clearly the connection between her life trajectory and participation in the movement.[5] I use anonyms in order to avoid the identification of the informants.

In the following three sections I show how the activists, particularly Kimoto, obtained the interpretive framework to link their life experiences with the internment experiences of the previous generation and the reparation movement. The second section looks at the activists' growth process, and the third part deals with the process underpinning the reparation movement. Concluding remarks will follow.

Growth process of younger generation activists

Claimants of the Japanese American reparation movement

Reparation claims for the Japanese Americans were initiated in the 1970s by a handful of second-generation survivors who had a history of political activism. The wartime internment had been either unknown in the public arena or justified until the late 70s, whereas the activists and some researchers were certain about the injustice. The reparation claim was strongly supported by the younger generation activists, yet in its initial phases it faced strong opposition or indifference from many of the internment survivors. Influential and politically savvy members of the Japanese American community who were mostly former internees took charge of the political and legislative process. Mobilizing the Japanese American community and obtaining diverse support were, however, carried out to no small extent by members of the younger generation (Tsuchida 2008). The movement gained momentum in the 1980s and accomplished reparation in the 1990s.

Previous works on the Japanese American reparation movement paint a general picture of how the younger generation participated in the movement. Among the younger generation activists, most of the third generation Japanese Americans were post-Second World War baby boomers. They spent their teenage years in the 1950s and through to the mid-60s (Takezawa 1994). Although the economic and social status of the Japanese Americans had generally improved, and the younger generation Japanese Americans had attained higher educational levels than before, the third generation were uncertain about their full economic and cultural participation in broader society (Takezawa 1994; Takahashi 1997: 157–8).

The third generation's political activism was developed through their experiences of major social movements ranging from the Civil Rights movement and the anti-Vietnam War movement to the Free Speech and the Asian American movement of the 1960s and 1970s

(Wei 1993). Takahashi (1997: 162) explains the influence of the movement thus:

> [T]he rise of multiple social and political movements within the context of major international and domestic upheavals created a space for certain Japanese American youth, together with their Chinese, Filipino, and Korean American counterparts, to rearticulate their sense of identity...

How, then, did the Japanese American youth who became politicized come to think that they needed reparation some thirty years after the war?

The personal struggles to locate 'who I am'

Most of the founding members whom I interviewed were born shortly before and after the Second World War, and a few were born in the late 1930s. Their parents were Japanese Americans. Among them, Mary Kimoto was born in 1948 in Los Angeles to second generation Japanese American parents. The Kimoto family lived at that time in an area very near to Little Tokyo, a historical ethnic enclave for Japanese Americans.

Both of Mary Kimoto's parents were Japanese Americans, but they grew up in disparate surroundings. While her mother was born and raised in the US, her father was raised in Japan after his birth in the US. The Pacific War broke out after he returned to the US in his early twenties. The internment policy sent his family to one of the camps, while he was assigned to work as a Japanese instructor at the language school that was part of the Military Intelligence Services. After the war, he did not reclaim the properties that he had before the war, and he worked as a greengrocer in the market to support his family.

The Pearl Harbor attack also changed Kimoto's mother's life. When she was twenty-two years old, the internment policy was enforced. The FBI took Kimoto's grandfather immediately after the Pearl Harbor attack, and the rest of the family was interned in the camp.[6] Kimoto's mother worked as a housekeeper and nanny to support the family after her release. Following her marriage to Kimoto's father, she worked as a seamstress in a factory and clerk for a jewelry company in Los Angeles. As shown in the case of Kimoto's parents, due to the internment policy, the parents of founding members of NCRR lost their properties and were forced to engage in lower-skilled jobs than before the war.

To Kimoto, her mother seemed a typical *Nisei,* a second generation Japanese American, who put emphasis on assimilating into US society. She recalls that her mother would say to Kimoto and her sister 'when in Rome do as the Romans do' to emphasize the importance of 'fitting in' to US society to be successful. Kimoto construed it as '[to] become white.' As she grew up, Kimoto rarely heard about the internment experiences from her family. Her mother once said 'it [the internment] was not just a big deal,' but never mentioned it further. Kimoto did not further question her family regarding the internment experience as she recalls that she did not really understand what the internment was and she had no interest in Japanese American history when she was a child.

Growing up without knowing the internment camp history was common to other members of the NCRR. One spoke about the fact that he had never known of the internment camp until he learned of it at college.[7] Another activist found that his parents and grandparents were outraged when he asked them about the internment.[8] This is also a common pattern among third generation Japanese Americans (e.g. Kitayama 1993; Takezawa 1994: 141).

Defining 'who is American?': internalizing 'white-supremacy'

Defining 'American' seemed to preoccupy Kimoto's growth process. Influenced by her mother, Kimoto herself tended to regard behaving like a 'white' as the way to be successful. She first went to school in Little Tokyo where all of her fellow students were Japanese Americans. Although she was at the head of the class, she did not find it easy to intermingle with other students, because they tended to behave in a cliquey manner and she did not find it easy to fit in with them.

Her definition of American was constructed during her high school years, as indicated in her recollection that 'when I went to high school, I made a decision...try to be American.' She went to a high school where many of the students and teachers were white females. This situation made her feel that she had to 'leave the Japanese part' behind in order to 'fit in.' This meant she had to behave like 'a white.' Though knowing that she was an American citizen in terms of her nationality, this did not provide her with a sense of being fully American. She had believed that 'white was better and I had to fit in.'

While she understood she could not change her 'face' or 'look,' she thought she 'could change anything else, [that is,] the way I acted... the way I dressed, tried to be like them [that is, whites].' She internalized *white supremacy* and established it as a behavioral social norm.

Yet, Kimoto 'never felt quite equal to the other Americans [that is, whites]' in high school. She became gradually tired of and disappointed with acting like a 'white.' Moreover, recognizing the difference in social class accelerated her frustration. Many of her classmates were from the middle- or upper-middle classes. Their parents were medical doctors, lawyers, and even relatively successful actors, while her parents were in the lower-middle class, and worked at a food market and a dress factory.

It was also when she was in the high school that she began to feel a 'sense of embarrassment' about being Japanese American. As she first studied Pearl Harbor in a history class, she recalls that she was 'looking down at my desk, feeling very hot and very red.' She also said, 'I felt like everybody is looking at me,' as she was the only one having ethnic ties to Japan in the class.

Kimoto's growth process indicates that she defined Americans as 'white.' Moreover, she established a sense that her Japanese ethnicity was a definitive defect to becoming an 'American.' In other words, she perceived that her ethnicity was a negative symbol for Americans.

Identity conflict: 'Japanese' or 'American'

In the late 1950s and 1960s, the US saw colossal social changes fuelled by major social movements. These social movements also gradually influenced Kimoto's situation. Even while she was attending high school, she had the opportunity to listen to the civil rights activists who were members of the Student Nonviolent Coordinating Committee. At this time, she was not yet interested in the social changes. Rather, she was concerned about the search for her identity. Nevertheless, her search for identity at this time consequently connected her through collective actions with other Asian Americans and Japanese Americans at a later date.

Kimoto entered the University of California, Berkeley, in 1966, which became a focal point for the student movement of the 1960s and early 70s. After spending two years in college, she decided to study in Japan. She expected to find answers to her identity question 'who am I?' by doing so because since her high school days she had gradually begun to feel 'I couldn't fit in the United States.' Alternatively, the society to which she expected to belong was Japan.

In Japan, Kimoto exerted herself to be a 'Japanese.' She attempted to learn, not only Japanese language, but also Japanese social values and norms: she always considered how 'Japanese' should behave on every occasion and judged herself according to whether she acted naturally and rightly as a 'Japanese.' For her, to be a Japanese meant to eradicate from her what *an American* is.

However, the attempt to become a 'Japanese' perplexed and tired Kimoto. While forcing herself to behave like a 'Japanese' in the way that she considered that other Japanese people do, she found this difficult to achieve by the end of her stay. When she returned to the US after finishing her program in Japan, she still held the question of her identity in her mind. She was still eager to find the answer to this question, but at the same time was disappointed with the continuous pursuit of it. She recalls:

> ...I went to Japan, but the answer wasn't there. I was here [in the US] and the answer wasn't here. And I said...Where do I belong?... There was no answer.

The fact that there was 'no answer' to her identity question dejected her deeply, even almost depressed her for a short period of time. She was sometimes frightened when she saw people on the street from different racial groups than hers.

Kimoto's life history here points to the key in her attempt to identify herself. Identifying herself could be accomplished by identifying with either 'American' or 'Japanese.' The important thing was that, to her, 'being an American' and 'being a Japanese' were separate and conflicting concepts.

Identity acquisition through social movements

As Kimoto almost failed to locate her identity, the social changes drastically involving racial/ethnic minority groups also affected her life course. She returned to college in the US in 1969 at the height of the student activism of the 1960s period. The students protested against the Vietnam War and demanded free speech and the establishment of study courses on racial/ethnic groups. The student activism had a great influence on her and she swiftly became politicized. Kimoto, along with the other students, participated in rallies and demonstrations even when police officers were leveling guns at them.

This period was also the time of 'the ethnic revival,' when racial/ethnic minority groups gathered and asserted their own cultural and political presence against the mainstream hegemony. Asian, African, and Latin American students became involved in the activism initiating 'the third world strike' in 1968 (Umemoto 1989). Criticizing the white supremacy implicit in educational programs, they demanded the establishment of ethnic study courses in which they could study their own histories and social issues relevant to them. Some NCRR members were active participants in the Asian American and student movements. One of them, a UC Berkeley student at the time, also recalls that the social movements of the 1960s raised his awareness for the possibility of social change. He recalls that he was convinced that people could improve a society from the grassroots level with their collective effort, regardless of differences in social position.[9] The Asian American study course, along with other fields of ethnic studies, was established at several colleges at that time.

Even over thirty years later, Kimoto still remembers the impact that the Asian American study course had on her. It was in this course that Kimoto and some of the other students learned of the Japanese American internment experiences of which their grandparents and parents had hardly spoke. Not only Japanese American history, Kimoto was also able to study the historical experiences of Asian immigrants and their descendents in the US for the first time in her life. To her, it was '*our* history in the US.'[10] She interprets the influences of the Asian American movement and the study course thus:

> Asian American class changed my life, [and] changed my whole thinking. I thought I found my place, I know who I am, I know where I belong. And I want[ed] to make a change.

As Kimoto describes, the Asian American course could provide the linkage between her life and the history of Asian immigrants in the US. It enabled her to obtain a sense of belonging in the US social context. This was an identity formulated as an *American with Japanese ethnicity*. In this regard, she recalls that the components of the identity were neither 'American always equals white' nor 'Japanese from Japan.' Rather, there was a sense that both comprise equal parts of who she is. In this way Kimoto also came to realize the diversity of American society.

The Asian American movement and the study course led young Asian Americans to reconsider their racial/ethnic communities. This was true for Kimoto and some of the other members of the NCRR. She found the values and importance of the Japanese American community as the foundations from which to learn the history and culture of Japanese Americans. This was a radically new perspective, as she had long distanced herself from the community. With this new perception, she affirmed her ethnic community and formed networks with the other Japanese Americans. At this time, one of the other NCRR members started a social welfare organization supporting low-income members of the Japanese American community. This disadvantaged group was left behind in the ethnic town as many of the Japanese Americans climbed the social ladder and were suburbanized.

Kimoto's experiences in college decided her life course after graduation. In 1970, she started working for the Japanese American community. The activities she engaged in there eventually brought her to the reparation movement.

Participating in the reparation movement

Returning to community

The major social movements greatly affected most of NCRR's founding members. The experiences arising from these movements greatly impacted not only on their life course but also in terms of forming the framework that recognized the reality and concerns of their ethnic community. In particular, the framework with which to identify and understand community concerns developed more substantially when they became involved in community activities. The extent of the commitment varied from member to member, nevertheless most of the NCRR's founding members were concerned with or working for the community.

After graduating from college, Kimoto returned to Los Angeles at the end of 1970. She joined a community organization in Little Tokyo and lived with other young activists in a commune in order to 'put the whole life into the community.' The community organization she was involved in handled the multifaceted issues such as poverty and social welfare in the senior generation, and the problems of youth and housing.

Among the issues in the community, Kimoto was enthusiastically committed to solving juvenile delinquency and youth drug problems. To her, there seemed to be three factors behind the problem. The first factor she identified was the effects of pressures from stereotypes of Japanese Americans. In this regard, she particularly considered that 'the model-minority myth' created the pressure on youth. In the 1960s and 70s specifically, Chinese and Japanese Americans were labeled 'the model-minority' groups in US society, due to their seeming success in terms of income, education, and low crime rates. This label was later criticized from within the Asian American academic community and the broader communities because they thought that it would produce misconceptions and obscure the problems faced by this group. At the same time, however, the groups frequently accepted the 'model minority' in terms of issues of ethnic pride. Therefore, the pressure originating in this 'model-minority' label could be put on Japanese American youth from both outside and within the community. In Kimoto's understanding, some of the youth would take drugs to escape this pressure. She was concerned that young people who were considered unsuitable in light of the favorable image of Japanese Americans could be further alienated from the community. Moreover, she thought that once labeled 'deviant,' the youth were not given the opportunity to make their voices heard in their community.

The second factor was, according to Kimoto, that the lack of a positive model for identity might drive the youth to take drugs. Her concern about identity originated in her own experiences. She understood that it was caused by their parents' negative attitude toward the history of Japanese Americans, especially the internment experiences. In her understanding, the youth were exposed to the white hegemonic society and were not given the opportunity to affirm their own history. Kitayama's work (1993) shows that many of the former internees considered the internment experience a 'shameful' part of their history and were reluctant to talk about it to their children and grandchildren. This negative sense about Japanese ethnicity was implicitly passed on to the younger generation.

The third factor that Kimoto identified was the gender imbalance in the Japanese American community. She paid particular attention to the fact that many of the young Japanese Americans who died of drug abuse were teenage girls. She considered that this was because the girls were not treated as equal to the boys. From her point of view, women in the Japanese American community were still required to play a subordinate role to men. Moreover, she found that it was difficult for most of the women to speak of their problems by themselves. Kimoto was very influenced by the Asian American women's movement that played a significant role in the Asian American movement (Wei 1993: 72–100). At that time, the Asian American women's movement had only just started penetrating into the community. Kimoto found a patriarchal tendency even in the attitudes of her fellow male activists.[11] She recalls:

> ...Even in during the movement, in the 1970s...we had the women's group. Because the way that men were not that good...they sometimes made women do most of the paper work, answer the phones, [while] they [men] would be the speakers. But we [women] said, 'no, that's not right.' Women can speak, women can read, we are not just going to make coffee, doing [the] paper [work] and taking notes.

What Kimoto saw underlying the problems was silence and lack of affirmative identity. She and the other members attributed this vacuum to the unhealed internment experiences.

This conception was further reflected in the interviews with the other activists who founded NCRR. They remembered that one of the most serious problems was the passive and quiet attitude of the people in the community in the face of their struggle against various issues. At the time, some of the other members were working against the redevelopment plan of Little Tokyo initiated by the city government. Under the plan, the city government evicted low income Japanese Americans and dismantled their housing. The activists interpreted this eviction in the 1970s as a parallel experience to the wartime internment, in that Japanese Americans were forcefully removed from their residences without the opportunity to speak of their rights (Kitayama 1993: 47). One of the activists recalled that she had found that low-income people could not speak of their problems or protest against their situation by themselves, they rather remained silent and stoic. The activists saw the unhealed memory of the internment behind their attitude. They perceived that there was a fear that if they acted against the authorities, people could be targeted again as was the case during the Second World War.

The activists considered that the lack of an affirmative identity and the silence of the people were the major generational issues experienced by Japanese Americans. The activists framed the issues as an extension of the damages from the internment policy, whether the Japanese Americans directly had internment experiences or not. This was the framework that connected present and past experiences. Their interest in pursuing reparation grew stronger and they shifted their activities to moving the reparation movement forward.

From community activities to the reparation movement

In the mid-1970s, interest in the reparation movement slowly grew amongst the Japanese American community. Although the movement had not yet taken form and there was not yet community consensus about pursuing reparation, the younger activists increasingly considered the internment policy seriously. They revisited internment sites and held meetings to learn of the wartime experiences of first- and second-generation Japanese Americans. Kimoto and the other founding members belonged to this wave of young activists. In 1980, they formed the NCRR to concentrate on the reparation demand. According to Kimoto, what motivated them to form their own organization was to 'build the movement in the community.'

NCRR members placed importance on grassroots movements that emphasized community participation. Before they formed the NCRR, two organizations had previously been established. These organizations had also attempted to gather support from the community and had called for donations to send a lobbyist to Washington DC or to hire lawyers to fight for their cause. Conversely, NCRR members defined that participation in the movement was more significant than giving financial support to the movement's organizations. A member comments on the different levels of support and participation:

> ...[The] more important is to empower members of our community to say do more than just write a check...[B]ecause if you just write a check, you don't feel involved, you are supporting but not involving in the campaign. It's when you give a speech, or get your family sign up the petitions, or you're writing letters...you personally involved in [the movement]. And that's what NCRR was trying to do, to organize people, to empower the people, to share the stories, to get them be active in the campaign...[Y]ou don't have to have a lot of money. You don't have to be a lawyer. ...You don't have to have money, but if you really spend the time to mail out, sign the petitions, get your friend

do the things, make calls... that makes you a part of the redress campaign...What our role was to organize grassroots, to provide a vehicle for what role they can take in the campaign.[12]

The participation of the community meant that it was not only the influential or professional people representing the community, but those in the broader community were enabled to carry the movement forward by themselves. Kimoto and the other activists in the NCRR thoroughly stressed that reparation should be claimed by people from diverse social backgrounds.

Leading the reparation movement was the learning process undergone by members of the NCRR who had not experienced internment. Kimoto recalls, 'I am who I am because of what I went through. My history. I lived through the Civil Rights and the Third World strike.' The young activists vicariously participated in the wartime experiences of the previous generation though the reparation movement. This represented another way to connect the young activists to Japanese American history. At the same time, sharing the stories of the first and second generation was another process that allowed identification with their own history.

Concluding remarks

The Japanese American reparation movement emerged on the crystallization of the social changes of the 1960s and 70s. It greatly influenced Japanese Americans as a group as well as the other racial/ethnic minority groups. The impacts from political and cultural changes in society and individual struggles for affirmative identity align with the process of participating in the Japanese American reparation movement, as Kimoto's life history has revealed.

Kimoto's life history partially supports the portrayal of third-generation Japanese Americans described in earlier works (Takezawa 1993). Yet, one of the important points here is that Kimoto's identification process contains a process that relativises the definition of American. 'Having Japanese ethnicity' and 'being an American' had not stood in pre-established harmony. To Kimoto, 'being an American' had always meant being monolithically White, while having Japanese ethnicity was the factor that would exclude her from what an American is.

There were not many choices in Kimoto's identification process. Although some groups such as American Whites might enjoy 'ethnic options' (Waters 1990), for people of racial/ethnic minority groups there have been few opportunities to pick and choose (Nagel 1996). Even Kimoto's US citizenship was never enough to identify herself as an American. She knew she was born in the US and that her parents were also Americans by birth, yet the institutional facts did not provide the sufficient resources to constitute the meaning of her identity. When she blended the two facets and eventually established Japanese American identity after the process of identification, her identification as a Japanese American indicates that she internalized the diverse definition of what an American is.

The political activism of the 1960s and 70s based on rebuilding racial/ethnic identity provided the way to renew racial/ethnic identity in the communities of color in the US (Nagel 1996). Kimoto's story shows how this 'ethnic revival' affected individuals in fact. The Asian American movement and the ethnic study course enabled her to establish a firm sense of identity. She found a sense of belonging in US society, through participating in the movements and course that connected US history with the histories of racial/ethnic minority groups. She could thus rearticulate her presence within US history as well as the history of her ethnic group. This rearticulation enabled Kimoto and other young activists to reaffirm their identity.

At the same time this rearticulation process laid the foundation for building their interpretive framework to recognize the contemporary issues within their ethnic community, as shown in Kimoto's life history. This framework was founded on their views of the past, which were greatly influenced by the political activism of the 60s and 70s. The younger community activists framed the contemporary issues as continuous damages that originated in the wartime internment experience. Based on this interpretive framework, they also framed the subjects to claim the reparation: that is, the subjects could incorporate both those who did and those who did not experience interment, since victimization occurred both directly and indirectly. Therefore, the NCRR's emphasis on the participation of the community was also backed up by their definition of the subjects of the reparation movement. By including different generations, the reparation movement became a measure to solve the contemporary issues as well as a way to heal and correct past injustices.

The stories of Kimoto and young activists indicate how they acquired the experiences of past injustices they had never experienced directly. The combination of the personal struggle of finding identity, and the social changes facilitated by racial/ethnic political activism, made it possible to link the past injustices to their own present situation. Under these conditions, the past was not just someone else's experience any longer, but became their *own* experience. Their stories reveal one of the processes by which reparation movements for past injustices can mobilize those who are often alienated or removed from direct experiences of them.

Acknowledgments

This paper is based on a study conducted by the author between 2004 and 2008. I would like to use this opportunity to express my deep gratitude to Mary Kimoto and all the members of the NCRR who offered their assistance.

6 Reflexive Modernity and Young Muslims: Identity Management in a Diverse Area in the UK

Satoshi Adachi

Introduction

Two events in 2001—the terrorist attacks in New York and disturbances in Northern England—changed the meaning of the word 'Muslim' from a religious category to one which provokes cultural, psychological, and political reactions and insecurities among people. These events also influenced political discourse on social integration in the UK. Multiculturalism, the doctrine for social integration in the UK since the 1980s, was replaced by the idea of 'community cohesion,' based on common values and citizenship. The words community cohesion, for the first time, appeared in a governmental report that scrutinized the cause of the disturbances in Northern England in 2001 (Home Office 2001). This report found that the cause of the disturbances was the existence of 'parallel lives,' a situation whereby 'ignorance about each other's communities had been turned into fear, and even demonization. The result was intolerance, discrimination and, in extreme cases, violence' (Home Office 2004: 7). Since the publication of this report, a remarkable point is that the new catchphrase, parallel lives, has been used to refer to the problematization of the self-segregation of Muslim communities as a whole, while the direct cause of the disturbances in Northern England was provocations leveled by far-right groups toward Muslim communities (Campaign Against Racism and Fascism 2001). After the terrorist attacks in London in 2005, the idea of parallel lives became connected with the radicalization of young Muslims due to the fact that those involved in this event were young Muslims born in the UK.

Some politicians and mass media outlets tend to sensationalize when talking about young Muslims, for example, focusing on terrorism and extreme protective movements. Such portrayals of young Muslims are extremely problematic because they promulgate false representations of Muslims in society.[1] Contrary to some political and media discourses on Muslims, the majority of young Muslims reside in the UK without serious conflict. To understand young Muslims, therefore, it is more important to observe how they 'adapt to' British society rather than to identify ways in which they 'deviate from' it.

The purpose of this chapter is to examine how young Muslims manage their identities and adapt to British society through the analysis of interview data. I use 'reflexivity' as a key concept in the analysis to understand the effects of gender, culture, and informationization on young Muslim identities.

Previous studies

Muslim society and young Muslims in the UK have been actively researched in the last two decades. Early studies of ethnic minority in the UK focused on the idea of 'race' rather than the idea of 'religion.' The former concept has been used to highlight educational and institutional discriminations, especially against Africans (Rampton 1981; Department for Education and Science 1985). In the 1980s 'Muslim' as a religious and cultural category gained public attention. The increase in the number of immigrants in the 1960s encouraged political activism amongst ethnic and religious minorities and resulted in multicultural movements in the 1970–80s. Multiculturalism enhanced the social and political presence of the Muslim community in the UK. Numerous studies were conducted to grasp the rise of the Muslim political movement and to understand the practices and problems of multiculturalism (Baringhorst 1992; Hilo 1992). In the 1990s, Muslims were discussed from the perspective of gender as well as education and class (Burlet and Reid 1998). Although these works on Muslims perceived them as a cultural category, they seldom address issues concerning the conflict and reconciliation between Muslim identities and British society.

The two events in 2001, mentioned above, directed public attention toward young Muslims and their social positions in the UK. Reviews of the disturbances in 2001 revealed that young Muslims were alienated from both British society and the broader Muslim community (Kundnani 2001). Phillip Lewis (2007) criticized, for example, Imams and Muslim communities for not trying to understand wider society and not tackling problems impacting on young British Muslims. As a result, according to Lewis, radical groups such as

Al'Qaeda had compensated for this void in young Muslim identities. Through a collection of interviews (Alam 2006) and a novel (Alam 2002), Yunis Alam depicted a situation where young Muslims could not position themselves and their identities in a positive manner, both in British society and in the Muslim community. These works made people aware of the importance of hearing the voices of young British Muslims. Muslim communities responded to these messages and started to tackle some of the problems faced by this group. It is reported, for example, that several Muslim organizations have made attempts to recognize the role of professionals and online self-help groups managed by the young Muslims (Ahmed 2009; Institute of Community Cohesion 2008: 23).

These discussions, occurring since 2001, are significant in that they act to counter political discourses intending to directly connect Islam's values to terrorism in addition to elucidating the various institutional difficulties faced by young Muslims. These previous studies, however, contain two key limitations, practical and theoretical. First, these works tend to exhibit excessive interest in the cultural or psychological conflicts of young Muslims. Due to this fact, some studies, especially those conducted by Islamic societies, seek to transform their analyses into political power to improve the social positions of Muslims. These trends and motivations result in studies overlooking the issue of how young Muslims manage their complex identities and adapt to British society in a contemporary setting. Second, previous studies lack a theoretical framework that facilitates the research of young Muslims from a post-modern perspective. The identities of contemporary young Muslims are heavily influenced by globalization and informationalization as post-modern structural factors (Ameli 2002), as well as by class, gender and ethnicity as modern structural factors. The aim of this chapter is thus to interpret the identities of young Muslims using post-modern theory.

Reflexive modernity and the identity of young Muslims in the UK

If we summarize the limitations of the previous studies on young Muslims and their relations with British society in one phrase, it would be a 'lack of a coherent theoretical perspective to describe the complexities of their identity management.' In order to overcome such limitations, I adopt the identity theory of reflexive modernity developed by Anthony Giddens and Ulrich Beck.

Giddens defines reflexive modernity as 'post-traditional society.' By post-traditional society, he does not mean a society in which tradition disappears, but rather he indicates one in which 'pre-existing traditions cannot avoid contact not only with others but also with many alternative ways of life' (1994: 96–7). Post-traditional society makes it difficult for people to establish a stable identity, because there are various authorities and rules for people to follow, and therefore 'the biography the individual reflexively holds in mind is only one "story" among many other potential stories that could be told about her development as a self' (Giddens 1991: 55).

Post-traditional society entails two consequences for people's identities. The first is 'individualization.' According to Beck, this word refers to the fact that the increase in flexibility in society, as a result of globalization, marketization, and informationalization, breaks the assumption that people could have 'in-dividual' identities, and rather demands that people have a divisible identity in order for them to adapt to a complex and flexible environment (Beck 1986: 127–38). In reflexive modernity, identity is no longer an obvious and indivisible thing, but is a subject to be achieved through the effort of individuals according to each life course (Giddens 1991: 75). Second, in post-traditional society, traditions as a resource of identity *'only persist in so far as they are made available to discursive justification'* (emphasis original, Giddens 1994: 105). Traditional conventions or rules are, thus, required 'to "explain" and justify themselves in a manner (...) to enter into open dialogue not only with other traditions but with alternative modes of doing things' (Giddens 1994: 105). In other words, people's identities and traditions in reflexive modernity must be redefined incessantly through personal reflections of experience and dialogue with society.

The identity theory of reflexive modernity is useful to analyze the identities of young Muslims in Western countries, due to the following two situations confronted by this group. First, since the terrorist attacks in New York in 2001, Muslim communities have been obliged to explain their religion to wider society to promote a better understanding of Islam. In particular, young Muslims feel a need or experience pressure to continue dialogue with other communities and their friends in order to foster positive recognition from the whole society and create positive identities as Muslim (Ahmed 2009: 71).[2] Second, young Muslims who were born or grew up in the UK have a reasonable expectation to join British society with equal rights on par with those of white British. Hence, they sometimes feel that some traditional conventions function to prevent them from accessing equal opportunity in this social context. To adapt to British society, they also need to negotiate with their ethnic community about social participation (Dwyer and Shah 2009). Young Muslims, therefore, should be motivated to manage their identities in relation not only to British society but also to their cultural or religious communities. These kinds of situations force young Muslims to develop a reflexive consciousness.

Research design: semi-structured interviews with young Muslims in Foleshill, Coventry

For the purposes of this paper, I draw on data taken from interviews I conducted with Muslims living in Foleshill, one of the electoral areas of Coventry in the UK. Coventry is a city located in West Midland and developed in the late 19th and early 20th centuries as an industrial area, focusing on motor vehicle manufacturing—Opel, BMW, Ford, and Jaguar plants were situated there. Coventry, like other industrial cities, experienced a significant influx of migrant workers following the Second World War due to labor shortages during the recovery period and the economic boom (Thoms and Donnelly 2000). This city also attracted a lot of immigrants from the new Commonwealth countries, in which the majority of the population were non-white— for example, Bangladeshi, Indian, and Kenyan. In 1981, Coventry was home to 17,738 people born in the new Commonwealth and Pakistan (total population was 274,044) (Coventry City Council 1986). According to the 2001 Census, the non-white population in Coventry represented 16.1% of the total population (the UK average is 7.9%). The majority of these immigrants were from Asian origins: Indian, 8.0%, Pakistani, 2.1%, and Bangladeshi, 0.6%. The Muslim population stood at 3.9% (11,733) and was preceded by Sikh (4.6%). Foleshill, where this research was conducted, is the most diverse area in Coventry. According to National Statistics data in 2001, the white population in Foleshill was below 50% of the total population and the Asian population comprised 48.3%. Coventry is, therefore, called a 'super-diverse' area, which means that the sum of the ethnic minorities surpasses the white population. Moreover, according to the 2007 index of Multiple Deprivation, Foleshill is the most deprived area in Coventry. This is reflected in the class position of the informants' parents.

From September to November in 2009, I conducted interviews with 13 young Muslims ranging in age from 18 to 25 who lived in

Coventry. I adopted a one-to-one, semi-structured approach and used an IC recorder for the interviews. Each interview ran for 80 to 120 minutes. Informants were composed of young volunteers from a community organization, young men I met in a park, the children of some students in an ESOL (English for Speakers of Other Languages) class, and friends of the above informants.

Table 6.1 shows the attributes of informants: seven of the informants were female and six were male; almost all informants were students in university, college or sixth form, and three were employed; most of the informants were Asian, but those from African and Middle Eastern backgrounds were also present, as well as those of mixed Asian and White descent; all informants were either first- or second-generation immigrants.

Individualization: selection and adaptation

There are two main arguments on young Muslims in political discourse. One proposes that young Muslims have recently been becoming more exclusive, and the other refutes such statements. In 2005, Trevor Phillips, who was Chair of the Committee for Racial Equality, gave a lecture titled 'Sleepwalking to Segregation.' In the lecture, he warned; 'we are a society which, almost without noticing it, is becoming more divided by race and religion' (Phillips 2005). He gave his opinion on the basis of YouGov, an Internet-based data survey funded by the Government. That data found that ethnic minorities, especially Asian Muslims, became more exclusive.[3] However, the Citizenship Survey, also a state-funded data survey, highlighted a different situation for young Muslims. According to the data of 2008–9, the younger generations from all ethnic groups including young Muslims are more engaged than ever before with those of different backgrounds (Communities and Local Government 2009: 15–6). The question remains as to whether or not young British Muslims have become exclusive in reality.

Friendship

Concerning the above contention, I asked informants about their friendships and the criterion they employed when they made friends. The informants' responses indicated that they do not have any difficulty in making friends with those of different backgrounds:

Table 6.1: Social attributes of informants

Name	Sex	Position	Qualification	Ethnicity	Generation
Yakoub	Male	Student	University	Asian	Second
Abdul	Male	Employed	College	Middle Eastern	First
Naseem	Male	Employed	College	Asian	Second
Sara	Female	Student	College	Mixed	Second
Shazia	Female	Student	College	Mixed	Second
Alia	Female	Student	College	Asian	Second
Shabid	Male	Student	Graduate	Asian	Second
Nazma	Female	Student	College	African	First
Yasmin	Female	Student	College	African	First
Wajit	Male	Student	Graduate	Asian	Second
Sultana	Female	Student	College	Asian	Second
Rahan	Male	Employed	Secondary	Asian	First
Nadia	Female	Student	University	Asian	Second

> Alia: I have a lot of different multicultural friends. And then, they like a, I have Muslim friends come from other countries as well, and like from Africa, Holland, and our country also.
> Interviewer: Is it not difficult to get along with such kind of people?
> Alia: No, it is not difficult at all. It's quite easier actually.

The informants were born and raised in a culturally diverse environment and communicate with each other in English as a common language. It is not difficult, therefore, to imagine having friends from different backgrounds in this context. One informant even claimed that 80% of his friends were non-Muslim (Shabid). Several of the informants often visit parks to play football after praying in the Mosque on Fridays and meet various types of young men there; for example, Asian Sikh, Turkish refugees, and overseas students. They use the word 'international' to express their football team's characteristics (Yakoub, Sultana) due to the diversity of its members. According to my informants, religion, ethnicity, and language are irrelevant when they are on the football field.

Some quantitative data verify that social contact in diverse areas like Foleshill have the effect of reducing people's prejudice. The Citizenship Survey in 2003, for example, demonstrates that those who live in diverse areas tend to have a weak recognition of 'racial prejudice in the UK' (Trikha 2004: 63–4). This result partly stems from the fact that such diverse areas promote not only group contact but also personal interactions. As research in psychology has shown, personalized contact can reduce prejudice (Gaertner and Dovidio 2000), while there is no linear relationship between levels of diversity and positive racial relations in the UK (Commission on Integration and Cohesion 2007: 28–31).

Some informants emphasize the significance of personalized standards for their friendships. An informant said; 'I don't matter about religion (...) Person is good or not, that's it' (Abdul). The following argument of Naseem demonstrates the interesting effect of personalized contact with those from different backgrounds.

> Naseem: Making friend is easily, even if this person doesn't like Pakis. He became friend of me. In a sense, I realize people are not racist (...) once he becomes close to me, he respects to me. He doesn't see me as Pakis or Muslims.

Naseem shows that personalized contacts make it easy to keep good relations with people even when they have racial or religious prejudices. It is possible that differences of race, religion or sect within Islam are not always irrelevant in terms of sociability. For example, Sunni and Shia groups within the Islamic community sometimes exhibit hostility toward each other. Yakoub mentioned, however, that it would not be an issue if they became friends before knowing which sect they belonged to. It is more natural to become friends before knowing each other's background. These remarks from informants illustrate that their friendships are highly personalized.

Islam and alcohol

Although informants claim that they get along with those from different backgrounds, they have other concerns regarding the different customs of those from Islamic countries. One of the cultural problems experienced by young Muslims is alcohol consumption. Consuming alcohol is, as is well known, a taboo in Islamic society. The *Qur'an* states; 'The Shaitan only desires to cause enmity and hatred to spring in your midst by means of intoxicants and games of chance, and to keep you off from the remembrance of Allah and from prayer' (the *Qur'an* 5.91). Muslims in general avoid drinking because it impedes consciousness and prevents them from keeping faith in God. In fact, almost all informants exhibited a negative attitude toward alcohol.

> Abdul: I think it is rubbish. Drinking is not important for them [that is, Muslims]. Drinking kills them. So that's why Muslims don't like it.

It is not easy for young Muslims, however, to avoid alcohol in the UK where drinking is regarded as a social norm by many. Some informants refer to the existence of 'peer pressure' in this regard. Sara said; 'Drinking is a norm in this country. All young drink to live.' The increasing complexity within Muslim society also provides young Muslims with occasions when they are present while others are consuming alcohol. Shazia, who is of mixed white and Asian heritage, mentioned, 'My father's family drink alcohol because they are not Muslim.' How do young Muslims manage such situations and evaluate their friends and relatives who drink?

> Alia: One of my friends, she is Muslim, and she's started drinking. Yeah, and I didn't like it. But I just said "ok, you do the way you want to do." But I just don't wanna get involved (...)
> Interviewer: Do you know why she started to drink?
> Alia: She is just wanted to have fun with other people, and because she wanted to try it something new.

Alia tries to avoid drinking. She does not, however, hate and renounce those who drink alcohol even if they are Muslim. Rather, almost all informants are tolerant toward their friends' drinking habits to the extent that it does not involve them and is not excessive. Informants even recognize friends' drinking as a personal choice. For example, Shazia stated; 'I don't do, I don't drink personally. One of my family will do. It just, it just, I've just seen something. You have, you have brown eyes. I have green eyes. You drink. I don't. It's just a difference.' Although drinking is an important taboo among Muslims, it does not break friendships in this social context.

Young Muslims manage their relationship with alcohol in various ways. Shabid, for example, said;

> Shabid: To be honest, I have drunk. I don't think it because of pressure. I wanted to try myself to see why is it about, why, why do people, why was such a culture that depends on alcohol. I tried it, although it's nothing I enjoyed it (...) Fine, I'm not sure pressure is right word. I'm not sure peer pressure. You must more adapt. You adapt in the way of that. Sometime you don't want to do. But you almost like it. You do normally so. It's not big issue. It's not a taboo subject.

In this response, Shabid admits that he has consumed alcohol not due to 'pressure' but because of 'adaptation.' The word adaptation is used by Shabid to express that his drinking comes from his will, not from external factors such as peer pressure. Although he is satisfied with being Muslim and has the intention to become a good Muslim, he thinks that this is not contradicted by his alcohol consumption. For some young Muslims, drinking is recognized simply as an issue of individual choice. This means that the extent of commitment to Islam and associated practices is perceived as an issue of individual choice, even though conversion from Islam is unlikely.

Differentiation between religion and culture

The concepts of 'adaptation' and 'choice' are deeply connected as all adaptations are conducted selectively. What makes adaptation and choice possible is the operation of 'differentiation.' The statements of informants suggest that they differentiate some Islamic teachings, which must always be followed, from others which need not always be kept. On the basis of this differentiation, informants can adopt some Islamic teachings as components of their identities and adapt to British society.

To explore the importance of differentiation, it is helpful to observe informants' attitudes towards some traditional conventions. Almost all informants complain that the older generation tries to impose too many restrictive conventions on the younger generation.

> Nazma: Old generation are very strict, they are very strength. And the old generation, they had arranged marriage. They got marriage very young, they got marriage under twelve, fifteen. But this generation, you know, although a Muslim, we want to have a job. And you wanna work as well. But in the old generation, they want to stay at home, cook, clean, have babies. But now we wanna have job as well. Yeah, and we wanna work, we want to work with everybody. You know, the old generation, I think they couldn't work with men. But now it's not a problem. So I think the old generation, they don't like the new generation. But.
>
> Interviewer: But?
>
> Nazma: Yeah, they don't, they don't, the old generation wants the new generation to be like them, do like they did. But it does not happen. Things changed.

Informants, of course, respect family ties and enjoy ethnic culture like their parents. As found in the statement of Nazma, however, they tend to be critical of some of the ethnic values and conventions. The greatest interests in their lives are study and career, unlike their parents, and informants fear that some ethnic conventions could prevent them from having the career they desire.

In spite of such laments over traditional conventions, all informants admit a sense of pride in their Muslim identities without any hesitation. When I asked them about the most important thing concerning their identities, for example, one informant said: '100% being Muslim' (Yakoub). Sara stated: 'I think, to be honest, obviously every day. So where I walk around and discuss, it is constant reminder.' If informants are strongly committed to their Muslim identity, what do their criticisms of some of the traditional values and conventions mean?

To answer this question, it is crucially important to realize the distinction between religion and culture, introduced by informants. They clearly differentiated between Islam as a religion and their ethnic cultures.

> Naseem: I said to mum like "I can't do arranged marriage," only because modern people believe in love marriages. So if I do find a girl only because I choose her for myself (…) it's [that is, arranged marriage] not religion, by the way. It's culture.

Naseem, who is Pakistani, refuses his mother's suggestion for an arranged marriage based on the logic that this form of marriage does not have any relationship to faith in Islam. Differentiation between religion and culture is the most significant strategy used by young Muslims to adapt to British society and is a line more clearly taken by female informants, who are under the influence of strict ethnic cultural rules, than male informants.

> Alia: I dislike a lot of traditional stuffs. But tradition is different from Islam. It is and that's the Bengali traditions that we have to follow and there are quite a lot. For example, when it's Eid day, some Muslims, they, they, whenever they see each other, they bow down to a person.
> Interviewer: Sorry, bow down?
> Alia: They bow down to a person like, they do that [that is kiss] to foot. And, and I disagree with that because I don't think they should do that, because you should only worship an Allah. That's why. And doing that, it shows, worshiping that person. We shouldn't do that. So and that is a tradition done in Bangladesh. And my family do that.

Alia's criticism of the 'allegiance to human being' derives from the teachings of Islam. The *Qur'an* prescribes believers to worship only Allah and banned the worship of any idols including Muhammad. Alia rejects some Asian conventions like wearing *sari* (Indian ethnic dress) because she intends to only follow the teachings of Islam.

Informants do not think that commitment to Islam necessarily contradicts the course of ordinary life in the UK. Rather, they recognize that both being Muslim and being British are well compatible with each other. For example, to the question concerning the position of women in Muslim communities, Nazma replied:

> Nazma: Now days people don't really go by the standard any more, like so many women who are, you know, company owners, or so many women are lawyers and doctors. So it's, it's what I think about. People, people changed, things changed. And I don't think it's a bad thing. I don't think that Islam as well, says "no, you shouldn't do that."

Nasma clearly differentiates the teaching of Islam from cultural oppression. She criticizes the latter because of the subjugation of women, yet supports the former because of the compatibility with the usual life course in the UK—attaining educational qualifications and building a career. Such attitudes of informants suggest that they negotiate the relationship with their cultural heritage and reflexively construct their identities through personal reflection on their life plan in the UK.

Who is truly British?: democracy and internationalism

As shown in the previous section, informants thought that it was possible for them to live in British society as a Muslim without serious difficulties. In spite of their statements, many people doubt, however, whether Islamic thinking and practices are compatible with democratic values and whether Muslims can be integrated in western countries. In the UK, this issue is revealed through the political arguments on Britishness. The word 'Britishness' is now a key concept for social integration, and has been associated with citizenship policy by New Labor to promote incorporation of minorities into British society. Britishness, as ex-prime-minister Gordon Brown put it, means 'being outward-looking, open, internationalist with a commitment to democracy and tolerance' (*The Guardian*, 12 November, 1998). Britishness, as expressing democratic values, has been used at times to suggest the disintegration of the Muslim community from British society, not least since the terrorist attacks in London in 2005 (Blair 2006). Is it right to suggest, as some politicians do, that young Muslims are 'inward-looking, closed, nationalists with a commitment to anti-democracy'?

Nick Griffin and democratic values

To scrutinize the above question, I asked informants about the appearance of Nick Griffin on a BBC talk-show program. Griffin is the leader of the British National Party (BNP), the far-right political party of the UK. He fell under the spotlight in the wake of his appearance on the BBC's *Question Time* on December 22 in 2009, one of the most authoritative political programs of the national broadcaster. The BBC decided to invite Griffin on *Question Time* after the BNP won a sizable portion of votes and two seats in the European elections in 2009. The BNP thus now represents to some extent a significant proportion of the public. The appearance of Griffin on *Question Time*, however, was quite controversial. Many could not accept that the BBC, which was expected to act in the interests of public welfare and social justice, gave Griffin a chance to air his racist opinions.[4]

This event attracted the interest of my informants, even though they did not usually pay particular attention to political issues. Their response to this event is relatively calm and tolerant.

> Alia: I thought and, at first, I thought that it seems a good way to see she or he says, although this should be interesting to watch. And, I thought, when he was speaking, some of stuffs of his things, it was a load of crap, to be honest. And I thought he, he doesn't know what it's all thought about. So I thought, but, it was good that he was on air, because, you know, people can understand what's happening.

The appearance of Griffin on the BBC was well received by informants. This is not just because they perceive that many will view Griffin's assertions as ridiculous, as Alia mentioned, but also because they feel that his appearance on the BBC is 'democratic' (Shabid). Informants stated that Griffin had a right to speak about the 'opinion he has' (Nazma), even if it is a racist one (Yakoub, Alia, Sultana). Informants' attitudes toward Griffin seem to represent tolerance, a characteristic Gordon Brown referred to as an expression of Britishness.

Informants' tolerant attitudes partly come from their school education. Many informants attend or attended X or Y secondary school, which teach religiously and ethnically diverse pupils including those from Asian, African-Caribbean, White, Middle Eastern, and recently Eastern European backgrounds. To manage such diversities, both schools prepare educational programs for encouraging various pupils to understand different cultures and religions. For example, X school provides a class on 'religious education' once a week, and, in that class, sets social issues closely related to the pupils as discussion topics; for example, immigrants, drinking, arranged marriage, and the Iraq and Afghan wars. Discussions in religious education help pupils foster an interest in larger society, to recognize the multi-facets of British society and to cope with cultural conflicts. As well, Y school, together with a community organization, organizes a 'global citizenship' program, which runs for an entire week on an annual basis. The purpose of the program is to help pupils find meaningful identities and pride in their ethnicities within British society. In that class, the concept of Britishness is used as a key tool to advance better integration of minority pupils in the UK, as advocated by New Labor politicians. However, the global citizenship program more strongly highlights the cultural diversity of Britishness, rather than the abstract values underpinning this concept, as some politicians have emphasized. Britishness in the program represents a multicultural, multiethnic, and multi-religious society. Pupils in Y school learn the new meaning of Britishness through unique ways: for example, a quiz game,[5] communication with pupils in Kenya via telephone, and talking with international university students.[6]

These programs contribute to the reduction of pupils' negative self-evaluation and can restrain potential aggressive reactions to social pressures such as racism and criticism of the Muslim community.

Internet and female Muslims

The public anxiety about undemocratic attitudes of Muslims comes partly from the image of the oppression of women as symbolized in the scarf and veil (Yuval-Davis et al. 2005). In fact, all female informants, as already mentioned, feel that some restrictions in their communities prevent them from integration in British society, although they perceive that these restrictions derive from ethnic conventions rather than from Islamic teaching.

The restrictions of traditional conventions tend to be imposed in a biased manner on female Muslims compared to male ones. Male informants are in fact permitted to stay outside or play football until nightfall. They, therefore, have a chance to interact with people from different cultures and to be socialized in larger society. On the contrary, female informants do not have such freedom and in general are expected to be at home with their families and relatives. Do these conventions, as some politicians worry, result in making young female Muslims narrow-minded and killing the chance for them to adopt democratic values?

Interview data indicate a different possibility: young female Muslims have the potential to develop a wider perspective even than that of their male counterparts. This advantage partly comes from the access to media cultures. Giddens states that in reflexive modernity the influence of the 'media' breaks through the established substantial and meaningful shields which sustained a particular social reality at one time, and brings various cultures and information into society; therefore, the Internet now constructs a new reality and provides a socializing function for the young (Giddens 1991: 26–7, 84–5).

Calling themselves 'addict' (Sara, Shazia) or 'junky' (Yasmin), female informants enjoy freedom on the Internet. For these informants, free access to the Internet is recognized as a kind of compensation for restrictions placed on them in the real world. The Internet provides female informants an opportunity to access more diverse cultural values and spaces. For example, Alia and Yasmin said that they participated in the 'cult' of Japanese animations, music, and dramas. Alia likes to listen to the music of Hikaru Utada, Mika Nakajima, and Ayumi Hamasaki, all Japanese musicians. As well, Yasmin often watches Japanese dramas and likes some Japanese actresses and actors; for example, Erika Sawajiri and Tomohisa Yamashita. They are also familiar with *manga* (Japanese comics) such as *Naruto* and *Doragon Ball Z*. They usually enjoy dramas, animations and comics of various countries via the Internet and Sky TV.[7]

Contact with media cultures facilitates female informants' socialization in a western country. Alia, for example, was hooked on a TV documentary on inspectors and has studied to become an inspector. Yasmin became interested in international business and decided to learn Chinese at university. These cases show that the influence of globalized media cultures and tools work beyond both local and national borders on the one hand, and beyond religious and cultural borders on the other. This results in the ability to be internationalists in a local setting.

Conclusion

The purpose of this chapter was to demonstrate how young Muslims in the UK, who are thought to have adopted different values and lifestyles from western culture, manage their multiple identities and adapt to British society. According to the interview data taken with young Muslims in Foleshill, being Muslim is well compatible with being British. They clearly differentiate between Islam as a religion and ethnic culture, although the old generation have confused the two, and are more strongly committed to following the former than the latter. In a sense, Islamic teachings are used as a measure to protect informants from some oppressive ethnic conventions and to justify their adaptation to British society. An important point is that they intentionally, in other words, reflexively, do so. Young Muslims who were born or raised in the UK hope to make it in that country as a Muslim. To achieve their dreams, they reflexively manage their identities and adapt to the various situations they face.

We cannot, of course, generalize from the results of this chapter because of the limited sample of informants in the study. In addition, the informants in this sample are relatively educated and, therefore, may have better hopes for the future than other Muslims. In spite of these limitations, this chapter has important implications. This research provides a different interpretation of young British Muslims from that presented in some political and media discourses. Although media discourses overtly or covertly tend to portray young Muslims in terms of radicalization, a large number of young Muslims, like my informants, live in the UK and struggle to find their position in society. Continuing to recognize Muslims as potential terrorists could feed the frustrations of young Muslims. It could even result in exacerbating the risk of their supporting radical Islamic groups. Rather, as Derek McGhee (2008) demonstrated, in order to prevent extremism, it is more essential to explore the causal relationship between governmental policy and the radicalization of young Muslims. This process might be caused not by Islamic teaching itself but by foreign policy or severe regulations placed on Muslims by the government such as the Iraq War and the discriminatory practice of stopping and searching young Muslims. What is now needed is not to enhance the reflexivity of young Muslims for their further assimilation into British society but to enhance the reflexivity of the government and media discourse to achieve recognition of Muslims as real members of society.

7 Status, Selection, and Exchange in an Okinawan Mutual Aid System

Masahiro Tsujimoto

Introduction[1]

How do people survive when they find themselves in difficult situations? Mutual aid is one form of collective action that people in need have mobilized to deal with certain circumstances. This chapter discusses one example of a particular form of mutual aid: the rotating savings and credit associations (ROSCAs) of women in Okinawa. Okinawa is an island group to the southwest of Japan. It was devastated by the ground battles in the Second World War, and was placed under US military administration until 1972. Okinawan people have struggled to survive waves of hardship through the years of US administration and the social disadvantages associated with living in relative poverty in a remote enclave of a war-torn country. ROSCA is a custom involving monetary exchange and is known to exist in various parts of the world (Ardener 1964; Ardener and Burman 1995; Geertz 1962), often functioning in situations of relative poverty to mutually assist members to financial gain. Utilizing ROSCAs has enabled many Okinawan women to overcome tough times and carve themselves a future. This study has the following three aims.

The effectiveness of the ROSCA system

The first aim is to examine the effectiveness of the ROSCA system. I first explain how monetary exchange works within a ROSCA. A ROSCA holds regular meetings of its members. At each meeting, members pay contributions to raise funds, which are received by a designated member. In this way, all members receive funds in rotation. If three people formed a ROSCA, it would work as follows. (Members are labeled A, B, and C and arrows indicate transfer of money.)

>   First meeting: (B, C) → A
>   Second meeting: (A, C) → B
>   Third meeting: (A, B) → C

At the first meeting, B and C would pay contributions to provide funds, and A would receive the sum. Once B and C receive their funds in a similar manner in the second and third meetings, the term finishes. In real situations, however, ROSCAs are formed with more members than three, and bidding or drawing lots decides the order in which members receive funds.

The ROSCA concentrates the money owned by individuals into the hands of a designated person. This arrangement has been proved effective in a wide range of situations. For example, Tsujimoto (2000, 2006) found that Japanese immigrants in Argentina employed the ROSCA for social mobility or to deal with emergencies such as natural disasters and illness. This chapter focuses on Okinawa, the homeland of many of the Japanese immigrants in Argentina, and examines the way ROSCAs are utilized by Okinawan women.

Peer selection

The second aim underpinning this research is to study peer selection within the ROSCA. An examination of the effectiveness of the ROSCA for social mobility and emergency assistance alone is not an adequate theoretical explanation due to the existence of the problem of non-contribution. There are two types of non-contribution: 'non-contribution before receiving funds' and 'non-contribution after receiving funds.' In this chapter, the term 'non-contribution' refers to the two types, and the term 'default' signifies the 'non-contribution after receiving funds' category alone. Default is an especially serious problem for ROSCAs. A member who has already received funds can increase her profit by defaulting. Therefore the ROSCA carries an incentive to default. Members who have not yet received funds suffer a loss when someone defaults.

For a ROSCA to remain viable, it must prevent non-contribution from occurring. Preceding studies have pointed to peer selection as a means to prevent it (Hechter 1987; Koike, Nakamaru, and Tsujimoto 2010; Tsujimoto 2005).[2] In this chapter, 'peer selection' refers to the exclusion of probable defaulters (e.g., transient people and people with no income) and those with a history of defaulting from a newly formed ROSCA. Barring the membership of those who have previously defaulted serves as a sanction against them. To ensure the effectiveness of peer selection, a ROSCA must be formed by people who know and trust each other.

However, it would be impossible to form a ROSCA if peer selection criteria were overly stringent. People in difficult circumstances—without wealth or a stable income—tend to fall into a situation where they cannot afford to pay their contribution. No one in a context requiring this form of mutual aid would be able to join a ROSCA if its peer selection criteria were too stringent. Therefore, peer selection also requires a certain level of forgiveness. This chapter particularly discusses peer selection and forgiveness found among the ROSCAs of Okinawan women.

ROSCA techniques

The third aim of this chapter is to study the techniques of the ROSCA system. In general, customs that have been cultivated over time in local communities can be highly complex and sophisticated. This is applicable to the ROSCA system, because its members employ a wide range of sophisticated techniques. Obviously there is no manual for the use of such techniques; the only way to master them is to participate in a ROSCA repeatedly in a local community where the custom has been handed down from one generation to the next. This chapter sheds light on ROSCA techniques used by Okinawan women and describes the life history of one member who has mastered them.

Study area

ROSCAs are called *moai* or *muē* in Okinawa. In the past the word *moai* was also used in referring to various sorts of cooperative labor and joint ownership, and is found in an account from 1733 in *Kyūyō*, a history of Okinawa. The reference to the ROSCA system in the account, however, is uncertain.

It is difficult to estimate exactly how many people participate in ROSCAs in present day Okinawa. A survey conducted in the early 1970s reported that about 60% of the respondents were members (Okinawa Kaihatsu Chō Okinawa Sōgō Jimukyoku Sōmu Bu Chōsa Kikaku Ka 1974). Reports in relation to the ROSCAs of Okinawa regularly appear in the mass media and publications—an Internet search will yield many web pages on the subject. Today's ROSCA members tend to emphasize the promotion of mutual friendship rather than the financial benefits that arise from participation.

The amount of each contribution generally figures in multiples of ¥10,000 (several hundred US dollars), except in special cases.

ROSCAs presented in this chapter operate within this range. Some ROSCAs have a promoter (*zamoto*) who is the key member of their operation. This member is responsible for the prevention of non-contribution and is afforded privileges such as the right to receive funds at the first meeting and preferential treatment regarding contribution.

The study presented here was conducted in Okinawa from 2003 to 2008. The subjects of this study were members of ROSCAs organized by a promoter who resided in the City of Naha on the main island of Okinawa. The promoter was Aiko, an elderly woman born in 1936.[3] Participant observation of a ROSCA organized by Aiko was conducted in 2003, and Aiko was visited and interviewed annually from 2003 to 2008. The following case study describes the ROSCAs organized by Aiko.

Case study

ROSCA meetings

The proceedings of a meeting are described below. Meetings are held at Aiko's home. The observations below were taken from a meeting held by ROSCA (1), one of the four ROSCAs run by Aiko to be discussed below. I visited this location at around noon on August 16, 2003 and conducted participant observation. The following is a summary of the record.

> Two of the members had arrived by noon and the rest arrived one by one and handed their contributions to Aiko. Aiko keeps some cash at hand on the day of the meeting so that absentees or a person who is unable to contribute the full amount do not disrupt the operation of her ROSCA. There were some absentees on this day whose contributions were paid by Aiko. Happenings like this were not disclosed to other members. Aiko considered that one of the functions of the promoter was to create a good atmosphere at meetings and members also stated that a good atmosphere was important for ROSCAs. Members were treated to a meal prepared by Aiko. The member who received funds paid for the cost of the meal. Aiko commented that good food was also important for ROSCAs. Members had a pleasant chat as they enjoyed their meal. They were free to leave as they wished. Aiko would not eat at all since she was nervous on the day of the meeting. All but one member had left by 3 o'clock in the afternoon, and Aiko finally relaxed and began to eat her meal.

According to Aiko, ROSCA meetings would usually start at noon, but several members would often come earlier to have a chat. Some members were pensioners who had no particular need for funds. ROSCA meetings thus provided a social and entertainment function for older people.

The numbers of ROSCAs organized by Aiko and members in each ROSCA varied from time to time. Changes in Aiko's ROSCAs between 2005 and 2008 are outlined below.

ROSCAs in 2005

As of July 2005, there were four ROSCAs organized by Aiko. These held monthly meetings on different days. Table 7.1 shows the four ROSCAs as of July 2005. The left-hand column shows eleven female members: seven of whom were in their 60s (including a member who is supposed to be around 60), two in their 70s and the remaining two in their 50s. Regarding occupation, three were retired and/or a housewife and the rest were in the trade business. Some of them used ROSCAs in order to acquire the necessary funds to support their businesses. Two lived at a distance from Naha, and the rest lived in and around the city.

Members of each ROSCA are marked by a circle in Table 7.1. Some members had multiple accounts in a single ROSCA. For example, a member who had two accounts in one ROSCA would pay twice the amount of contribution and receive funds on two occasions in the term. As noted in Table 7.1, some ROSCAs operated over many years. The longstanding ROSCAs restart a new term every time another ends. Each of the four ROSCAs is described in detail below.

ROSCA (1) used a bidding method to determine who receives funds. It is the longest standing ROSCA of the four, which had been running for about 22 years. The motive for its formation was Aiko's need to acquire funds to start a business. During the long life of ROSCA (1), several of its members have passed away. When members died after receiving funds, Aiko covered the loss that ensued without involving other members. Aiko stated that this kind of response was 'one of the secrets to the smooth operation of ROSCAs.' However, other members were apparently aware that Aiko had covered the loss.

ROSCA (2) had a predetermined order for receiving funds. If a member wished to receive funds at an earlier time than allotted, however, the order can be rearranged upon request. ROSCA (2) started about five years before the time of the study. The purpose

Table 7.1: ROSCAs as of July, 2005

Member	ROSCA (1) Formation:[a] About 22 years prior	ROSCA (2) Formation: About 5 years prior	ROSCA (3) Formation: About 4 years prior Closure: July 2005	ROSCA (4) Formation: About 1 year prior
Aiko	o	o	o	o
Rinko	o	o	o	o
Keiko	o	o	o	–
Minako	o	o	–	o
Noriko	o	o	–	o
Mariko	o	o	–	–
Kimiko	o	–	o	–
Tomoko	o	–	o	–
Takako	o	–	–	–
Tokiko	o	–	–	–
Naoko	–	–	–	o

Note: a = The years of formation are counted from the base year 2005.

of its formation was to assist Noriko, who was trying to raise funds without relying upon her son and daughter-in-law. A ROSCA was organized with Aiko as its promoter. From the outset, Aiko did not inform the other members that Noriko was short of funds.

ROSCA (3) used a system of drawing lots to determine who receives funds. However, this order could be rearranged by mutual agreement. This ROSCA started four years previously, when Keiko needed funds to renovate her shop. Keiko struggled to raise her children as a single mother. ROSCA (3) closed in July 2005. Aiko stated that she ended it because it had attained its objective of helping its members and she did not want to be in charge of too many ROSCAs at one time because it was hard work to prepare for them.

ROSCA (4) also used a system of drawing lots to determine the order of fund allocation. Just like ROSCA (3), the order could be rearranged by mutual agreement. ROSCA (4) started one year before. It was formed because Naoko had an urgent need for funds when two of her family members fell ill. Aiko phoned around and gathered enough members to form the new ROSCA in one day. Aiko did not inform potential members about Naoko's situation when recruiting them. Once ROSCA (4) was formed, Aiko advised Naoko to set aside some money daily to prevent non-contribution and covered any deficit when Naoko was unable to pay her contribution.

ROSCAs (2), (3), and (4) were formed for the purpose of assisting those who were short of funds. At the start, Aiko received funds at the first meeting, and then lent them to the person in need of funds. The borrower repaid Aiko when she received funds at a later point in the term. Since Aiko had multiple accounts in each ROSCA, she was able to receive funds on multiple occasions. Aiko kept the funds she received at the first meeting and sometimes lent some of this pool to those who did not receive funds as they were in need of them. Besides the exchange of contributed funds, members lent and borrowed funds according to personal arrangements. For example, a fund recipient might lend the funds to another member. Aiko commented that money was constantly circulating among members.

Changes up to 2008

Aiko dismantled her ROSCAs one by one after 2005 and started a new ROSCA from 2008. Table 7.2 shows the result of a follow-up study of the ROSCAs listed in Table 7.1. Since ROSCA (3) was closed in July 2005, the subjects of the follow-up study were members of ROSCAs (1), (2), and (4). In Table 7.2, the white circle indicates those who stayed until the closure of the ROSCA and the black circle signifies those who quit before the closure.

ROSCA (1) closed in October 2007. Looking at changes in its membership, Tomoko and Takako were members in 2005 and left before the end of the ROSCA. Naoko and Yuiko joined after 2005 but Naoko left before the closure. ROSCA (2) closed in February 2006. Its membership did not change. ROSCA (4) closed in April 2007. Its membership changes included Naoko who left before its closure and Keiko who joined at the time.

The three members marked by a black circle left the ROSCA for various reasons, but some did default due to business downturn or illness. Aiko covered the loss incurred by the other members due to default. She visited defaulters, but it was difficult to recover unpaid contributions.

Aiko mentioned the problems of interpersonal relationships and non-contribution as her reasons for closing ROSCAs (1), (2), and (4). Perhaps Aiko had too many ROSCAs and covered for non-contribution too many times beyond her financial capacity. Aiko stated that she wanted to consolidate them into one ROSCA.

Aiko started a new ROSCA as a promoter in 2008. After the closure of ROSCAs (1), (2), and (4), some people asked her to re-form

Table 7.2: Result of follow-up study

Member	ROSCA (1) Closure: October 2007	ROSCA (2) Closure: February 2006	ROSCA (4) Closure: April 2007
Aiko	○	○	○
Rinko	○	○	○
Keiko	○	○	○
Minako	○	○	○
Noriko	○	○	○
Mariko	○	○	–
Kimiko	○	–	–
Tomoko	●	–	–
Takako	●	–	–
Tokiko	○	–	–
Naoko	●	–	●
Yuiko	○	–	–

a ROSCA. Aiko stated that they wished to re-form a ROSCA because elderly people enjoyed going to ROSCA meetings. Some elderly people have no reason to get out of their home other than for ROSCA meetings. The new ROSCA was begun in 2008 with ten members. Membership details are not known, but it can be assumed that many of the members are former members of ROSCAs listed in Tables 7.1 and 7.2, considering the circumstances surrounding its re-formation.

Peer selection

Peer selection as explained by Aiko is summarized here. According to Aiko, adding new members increases the risk of a ROSCA breakdown. A new member may be added after an existing member passes away, but she must be referred by a friend. The new member does not receive funds until the latter half of the term. Those who intend to default usually want to receive funds at an earlier meeting. Those who stop paying their contributions after receiving funds cannot be forced to pay them but are barred from participating in other ROSCAs.

However, Aiko would cover for temporary non-contribution so that it would not become a problem for the group. Those who missed their contributions would repay the money to Aiko at a later date. Aiko contributed on behalf of a member at the meeting where participant observation was conducted. Aiko may cover instances of non-contribution of both those who have not yet received funds and those who have already received funds. Those who commit temporary non-contribution after receiving funds are not barred from participating in other ROSCAs.

Other members are also involved in peer selection. When the promoter proposes to add a new member, other members may oppose it if they have any doubt about the candidate's ability to pay contributions. Since the promoter is responsible for the prevention of non-contribution, some members state that they would only participate in ROSCAs organized by reliable promoters.

Life history of the promoter

The following is the life history of Aiko based on an interview conducted for the purposes of this study. Aiko was born in a southern farming village on the main island of Okinawa in 1936. Her mother was born in the same village in 1905 and married a cousin from the same village at age 16. The bride took a roll of cloth and two goats with her. The goats were to be her private property after marriage (separate from the husband's property, for the purposes of the wife's capital-building endeavors). Some time later, she returned to her parents' home and remarried another village man who was to be Aiko's father, and they went on to have six sons and four daughters.

Aiko's mother used to tell Aiko that life was 'very hard due to extreme poverty.' Once, one of Aiko's brothers was admitted to a teacher's college in Taiwan. Her family did not have enough money to send him there and her mother asked villagers to join a ROSCA. At the first meeting her mother received funds for her son's education. The ROSCA's membership was comprised of twelve farming households and held an annual meeting when they received income from sugarcane harvests for a term of twelve years. A feast was prepared for each meeting, and the member who received funds at that meeting paid the cost. Not all villagers were allowed into the ROSCA. The ROSCA was formed by those who 'knew each other's ways intimately' and sincerely wanted to 'provide mutual aid.' Because non-contribution would place a burden on other members, those who held only small acreages would not join a ROSCA, nor would they be invited to do so.

Toward the end of the Second World War, ground battles were waged in Okinawa, and many local residents were casualties. In the lead up to the Battle of Okinawa, Aiko was evacuated to hide in the northern mountains on the main island of Okinawa. Her mother put her children on a horse-drawn carriage to deliver them there. They staved off hunger by subsisting on nuts and crawfish. Adults descended from the mountains in the black of night to gather potatoes. Once the Battle of Okinawa ended, Aiko's family lived in a pig shed in a northern village for a while. They returned to the southern region after a time, but it was another six months before they could return to their own village. Aiko's father died in the Battle of Okinawa. Aiko said 'I am absolutely against war.'

Okinawa was devastated by the war and placed under US occupation. After the war, the people of Aiko's village took rice, potatoes and eggs to Naha City where they bartered them for daily necessities. Aiko's mother distilled spirits from potatoes and carried them around on her head for sale. They were hard pressed even to provide enough food for the family. Aiko had to drop out of high school and went to work at the US army base and also to Naha to work as a domestic servant. After that, she worked in shops in nearby villages.

Aiko married in her late teens. Her husband's family owned a civil engineering contracting business with dozens of live-in workers. Aiko was put in charge of preparing meals for them. She went to a cooking school and this experience proved fortunate later in life. She joined a ROSCA for the first time during this period.

Shortly after turning 30, Aiko left her marriage and opened a restaurant in Naha. She raised the necessary funds for her restaurant through a ROSCA. Aiko commented that the only thing she could rely on in those days was her prowess in cooking. After operating her restaurant at several different locations, she moved it to Naha's central business district. This restaurant became very popular, and she employed one assistant and began opening for breakfast. She did not have time to wash her frying pans during the busy lunch hour and had five going on the stove at the same time. She made concerted attempts to retain her customers by changing the menu daily and remembering the likes and dislikes of her regulars. She visited the Philippines frequently to buy bananas during this period.

Aiko participated in as many as fifteen ROSCAs at one time while she was running her restaurant. She was the promoter for some of these but not all. If ROSCA meetings were held at her restaurant, she would earn extra money from the sale of food and drinks to the members. Since her restaurant was in the central business district, the ROSCAs of company owners and managers were held there, of which Aiko was also a member.

Regarding a woman running her own business, Aiko commented that it would be 'really difficult unless she was very strong-willed.' For example, she once had a man brandishing a knife in her restaurant. Aiko raised her children while running her restaurant and did not have enough time to go and cheer for them at school sports carnivals and events. She looked back on this time and said 'poor children.' She would occasionally go out to drink on weekends but always came home while her children were asleep so that she would be there when they awoke in the morning.

Aiko ran her restaurant for fifteen years and stopped when she was in her mid-40s. She started a catering business in partnership in her late 40s, raising the funds to purchase a freezer van needed for transporting ingredients. Aiko handled most of the work in terms of the preparation and cooking of seafood. She was involved in the catering business for ten years or so and retired after turning 60 when she experienced some health problems.

Discussion

The effectiveness of the ROSCA system

The ROSCAs in this study function to help people survive tough times. The four ROSCAs listed in Table 7.1 were formed for the purpose of assisting those who were in need of business funds and those who had a sudden illness in the family. Members who run businesses raise necessary operating funds through the ROSCA from time to time. In addition to the exchange of contributed funds, ROSCA members lend and borrow funds according to personal arrangements. Members engage in flexible lending and borrowing practices. Aiko described this situation as 'money was constantly circulating among members.'

The ROSCA system is also connected to the independent economic life of women. Some of the women of the ROSCAs listed in Table 7.1 raised their children by themselves while running their own enterprises. Aiko left her marital home when she was young, used ROSCAs to finance her businesses and raised her children on her own as described in her life history above. Aiko also mentioned that her mother owned private property. In the past, some of the women in the southern region of the main island of Okinawa owned private property separate from their husband's assets and utilized this capital through the ROSCA system (Noguchi 1969; Shihō Shō Chōsa Bu

1942). As mentioned above, the ROSCA system has been associated with the independent economic life of women in historical record.

The ROSCAs discussed in this study were voluntarily formed and operated by women. No outsiders interfered with their operation. This is what makes the flexible exchange of funds and the independent economic life of women possible in this social context.

Peer selection

The ROSCAs mentioned in this study practiced peer selection. New members were limited to those who were referred by friends. Habitual defaulters who stopped paying their contributions after receiving funds were barred from participating in ROSCAs. However, peer selection allowed for a certain level of forgiveness. Firstly, ROSCAs were formed to assist those who were in need of funds. Those who were short of funds might not be able to pay their contributions, but were not necessarily excluded from ROSCAs. Only those who had no capacity to pay contributions at all were excluded. Further, those who were temporarily unable to pay their contributions could borrow money from other members. The borrowers would pay back to the lenders at a later date. This kept non-contribution from becoming a problem for the group. Temporary defaulters were thus not barred from participating in ROSCAs.

This level of forgiveness was required because very stringent peer selection criteria would stop those in need from accessing the ROSCA. Peer selection is necessary for the prevention of non-contribution, but no one can participate in a ROSCA if peer selection is enforced on an overly strict basis. A certain level of forgiveness is necessary for this reason, but excessive forgiveness could result in frequent defaults. The level of forgiveness is presumably adjusted to produce a proper balance in this trade-off.

ROSCA techniques

ROSCA members use sophisticated techniques. Peer selection, discussed above, was one of these, and the following also deserve to be mentioned.

The first is the special status of the promoter. The promoter is given the right to receive funds at the first meeting and preferential treatment with regard to contribution, but she is also obliged to cover any loss arising from defaults. In this way, members hedge against the risk of loss and the promoter pays close attention to her ROSCA's operation in order to prevent default. The second technique relates to the determination of the order of recipients of funds. Aiko allocated new members to receive funds in the latter half of the term in order to deter intentional defaulters from participating. Multiple methods were used for the determination of the order of rotation, including the bidding and drawing lots. One advantage of the bidding is that members can choose when they want to receive funds. However, Aiko was concerned that the amount of premium a successful bidder had to pay to the other members (a type of interest; the amount to be determined by bidding) might become too high. Conversely, drawing lots does not allow members to choose the timing of funds received, but this avoids the issue of rising premiums.[4] Thirdly, Aiko made an effort to create a good atmosphere at meetings. For example, Aiko would not tell other members that someone was unable to pay a contribution at a meeting. If they got to know of the existence of a non-contributor, they would start worrying about default. Aiko prepared delicious food so that a meeting would also function as an enjoyable social occasion.

As mentioned in her life history above, Aiko's mother had used the ROSCA and Aiko has been involved in ROSCAs continuously from her early years. Aiko learned the techniques of the ROSCA as part of her inheritance and has practiced them throughout her life.

Future challenge

Not everyone can operate ROSCAs effectively. It is a difficult task unless one hails from a local community with a history of cultivating sophisticated ROSCA techniques. Such techniques cannot be devised in a short period and one needs to participate in many ROSCAs over many years in order to master them. Consequently, the ROSCA would not be particularly appropriate in various minority communities in contemporary society. However, this does not mean that the ROSCA is not worth studying. The purpose of ROSCA studies is not to popularize the use of the ROSCA but to theorize the essential elements of the mechanisms for implementing mutual aid and apply this knowledge to contemporary society. The challenge for the future is to construct a concrete proposal about how the knowledge gained from the studies of the ROSCA system can be applied to contemporary society.

8 Cultivating Social Diversity and the Role of NGOs/NPOs

Kōichi Hasegawa

Introduction

How can we expand the cultural and social diversity of Japanese society? While President Barak Obama emphasized America's 'patchwork heritage' as a measure of its strength, a lack of such heritage can be considered Japanese society's weakness. Japan's regional diversity was probably more marked before the Meiji period. From this time, the country's equalization and homogenization progressed as a more centralized state system was developed. The expansion of socio-cultural diversity is a great challenge for Japanese society in this age of globalization. However, young people are becoming increasingly inward-looking. Some difficult issues are lying in the path of a move towards more ethnic diversity. Although some progress has been made with respect to women's participation in society, Japan's position on the international scale of indicators for women's social involvement has been falling in recent years. Now hopes for the development of social diversity rest on NGOs/NPOs, which have been increasing in number rapidly since legislation was passed in 1998. This chapter aims to identify triggers for the expansion of social diversity, examining NGOs/NPOs as the driving force behind Japanese civil society.

Patchwork versus monotone heritage

In his inauguration speech on 20 January 2009, President Obama of the US stated, 'Our patchwork heritage is a strength, not a weakness' and stressed, 'We are shaped by every language and culture, drawn from every end of this Earth.' The history of the US is of course full of painful experiences as he described: 'We have tasted the bitter swill of civil war and segregation, and emerged from that dark chapter stronger and more united.' The Obama administration itself had to fight a tough battle in the mid-term election of November 2010 as the Tea Party

Movement and other anti-Obama campaigns gathered strength. Yet, the acceptance of diversity is one of the most fundamental American values regardless of party affiliations and especially for liberals represented by Obama and his supporters.

The successes of immigrants are the driving forces behind the dynamic diversity of US society. There is an endless list of migrant success stories, with Obama himself, the son of an immigrant, being a prime example. In the IT industry, Sergei Brin, the co-founder and one of the CEOs of Google, is a first generation immigrant who was born in Moscow and came to the US at the age of six with his family. Jerry Chih-Yuan Yang, the co-founder of Yahoo!, is a second generation immigrant who was born in Taiwan and came to the US when he was two.

In contrast to America's patchwork heritage, Japanese society is characterized by relatively high homogeneity, which we may call 'monotone heritage.' The aesthetic beauty of monotone heritage is clearly found in traditional Japanese culture in the form of *sumi-e* (ink painting), tea ceremony and so on. In his famous essay *Inei raisan* (In praise of shadows), Jun'ichirō Tanizaki (1933) praised and elaborated the subtle beauty of the contrasting light and shade of a monotone heritage. However, this self-absorbed aesthetic world had been erased from Tokyo by the Great Kantō Earthquake even before Tanizaki wrote his piece in the 1930s; it was merely an afterglow that was disappearing from society. In fact, Tanizaki moved to the Kansai region (the western region of the main island of Japan) after the Great Kantō Earthquake in 1923.

The beauty of monotone light and shadow was the essence of Japan's traditional arts and aesthetic sense intuitively captured by the eminent novelist, but this does not indicate that Japanese society was in a strictly monotonous state even in those days. It is likely that Japanese society was more culturally diverse in the pre-modern period before the establishment of 'modern Japan' as a centralized state during the Meiji period. Yoshihiko Amino (2000) has studied the medieval history of non-farming nomads with a special focus on medieval craftsmen and entertainers. Norio Akasaka, influenced by Amino's view, has conducted a reevaluation of hunter-gatherer culture. Akasaka (2007) proposes the idea of 'multiplex Japan' by quoting Tarō Okamoto, who emphasized the significance of Jōmon culture[1] and argued that 'Japan is a complex, multi-layered structure.' Eiji Oguma (1996) has revealed that the theory of 'mono-ethnic Japan' was advanced when the state renounced colonialism following the Second World War. Thus, the suspicion that the cultural homogeneity of Japanese society developed more in the process of modernization than in pre-modern times is particularly pertinent when comparing modern and contemporary Japan. We must remember to retain skepticism toward the idea of a monotone heritage.

Japan's declining international competitiveness

The stagnation of Japanese society, which has become increasingly obvious in the face of globalization in recent years, is partially attributable to decreasing social dynamism and rising stasis. One example of this stagnation is a decline in international competitiveness. There are two major ranking systems for international competitiveness, one of which is released by IMD (International Institute for Management Development) in Switzerland. As shown in Figure 8.1, Japan ranked first from 1990 to 1992 and between second and fourth from 1993 to 1996, but the ranking dropped sharply in 1997 and since 1998 Japan has been floundering in the twenties, ranking 27th in a field of 58 countries in 2010. It ranked lower than China and Korea, which occupied the 18th and 23rd positions respectively, as shown in Table 8.1. The rankings are determined based on which countries provide the environment most conducive to the competitiveness of enterprises. In 2010, Japan came 39th in the category of economic performance, 37th in government efficiency, 23rd in business efficiency and 13th in infrastructure, and gained an overall ranking of 27th.

Figure 8.1: Japan's IMD international competitiveness ranking

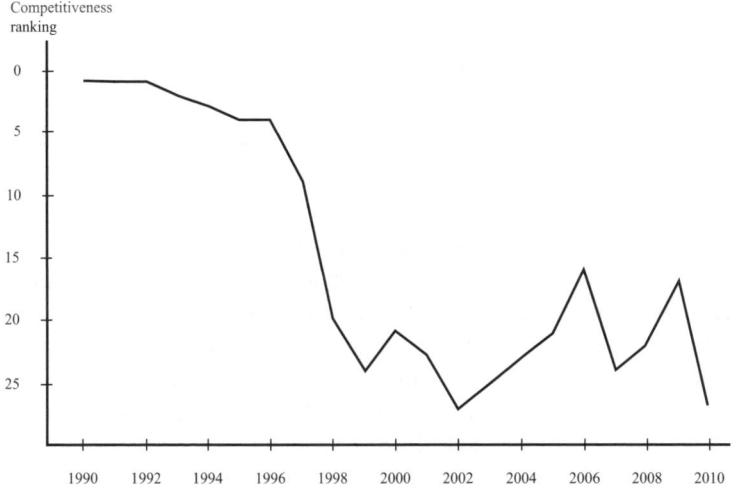

Table 8.1: Top 30 in the IMD international competitiveness scale (2010)

1. Singapore
2. Hong Kong
3. USA
4. Switzerland
5. Australia
6. Sweden
7. Canada
8. Taiwan
9. Norway
10. Malaysia
11. Luxemburg
12. The Netherlands
13. Denmark
14. Austria
15. Qatar
16. Germany
17. Israel
18. China
19. Finland
20. New Zealand
21. Ireland
22. UK
23. Korea
24. France
25. Belgium
26. Thailand
27. Japan
28. Chile
29. Quebec
30. Iceland

While Japanese society's relatively high homogeneity has long been regarded as a factor contributing to its stability, social integrity and low crime rate, its negative aspects such as rigidity and low vitality have been highlighted by the emergence of globalization. In the IT industry, for example, Japanese companies traditionally known for their technological strength have lagged well behind Nokia, Apple, Google, and Korea's Samsung in the development of mobile phones and smart phones.

The rise of hereditary politicians and the leadership crisis

The declining social dynamism of Japanese society is clearly illustrated by the increasing number of hereditary politicians and the resultant deepening of the leadership crisis. Currently, 42% of the members of the National Diet belonging to the Liberal Democratic Party (LDP) are reportedly politicians who have inherited their electoral base from their parents. The proportion was 32% before the 2009 general election, but the LDP's crushing defeat in the poll resulted in a 10% increase in the number of hereditary members. Although public opinion during the election campaign was firmly against hereditary politicians and some even proposed a restriction on their running for office, hereditary politicians were able to do relatively well despite their party's loss due to their strong electoral base.

All eight prime ministers in the last fifteen years from Ryūtarō Hashimoto, sworn in in January 1996 to Yukio Hatoyama, who resigned in June 2010, were either hereditary or near-hereditary politicians. Strictly speaking, the father of former Prime Minister Mori was the mayor of one of the towns in Mori's electorate and not a Diet member. Nevertheless, Mori can be regarded as a hereditary politician because he inherited his strong electoral base from his father. Yukio Hatoyama did not directly inherit the electoral base of his grandfather, former Prime Minister Ichirō Hatoyama, one of the influential leaders of postwar Japan, and he sits for a different constituency. However, he is the first son of the well-known and very wealthy Hatoyama family and his father was a member of the Upper House and he can thus be considered a typical hereditary politician.

Out of four recent prime ministers from Shinzō Abe to Yukio Hatoyama, who all resigned within one year of appointment, three were the grandsons of former prime ministers and one was the son of a former prime minister. All four came to office with great expectations and high cabinet approval ratings immediately after inauguration. All four also came unstuck within a short period of time and were compelled to resign without any notable successes. Except Asō, who was forced to resign after losing a general election, the remaining three voluntarily relinquished power. Their actions highlighted the feebleness of 'blue-blooded politicians' in the mind of the nation, as well as surprising both Japanese and overseas observers. Tarō Asō, who prided himself on being the grandson of Shigeru Yoshida, the most influential political leader who successfully led a recovering postwar Japan, (he made this his greatest selling point), often invited sniggers by misreading rather simple words and farcically personified the stark contrast between the greatness of the grandfather and the pettiness of the grandson. The LDP fought the Lower House election under Asō's leadership miserably and lost power.

Great hopes were placed on Yukio Hatoyama, who defeated Asō and accomplished a political power shift as the leader of the Democratic Party of Japan. However, the real power was in the hands of Secretary-General Ichirō Ozawa, a hereditary politician and, despite the gallant slogan of 'political leadership,' many mishaps typified by Hatoyama's handling of the proposed relocation of the US military base in Okinawa caused disappointment and the cabinet approval rating continued to fall rapidly.

The exceptionally high proportion of hereditary politicians and the pattern in which a succession of the sons and grandsons of former prime ministers ascend to the premiership only to lose it for their 'incompetence,' are rather unusual for a developed democratic nation and indicative of the fact that greater importance is attached to the pedigree and 'high birth' of a politician rather than his or her own skills or abilities. Thus Japanese politics is exhibiting a serious case of leadership crisis and losing its international influence year after year. The state of the Japanese government demonstrates most obviously the danger of decreased diversity.

Inward-looking youth

In Japan, there are concerns about the 'inward-looking tendency' of young people in the face of globalization. Young people used to be considered the driving force for diversity and dynamism, free from fixed ideas and preconceptions, but this is not necessarily the case with today's Japanese youth. According to the 2010 White Paper on International Trade (Keizai sangyō shō, 2010), the number of people who studied overseas in 2007 was 4.4 persons per 10,000 people, only one fifth of Korea's 22.1 persons. In absolute terms, the number was 54,000 persons in Japan, about half of Korea's 107,000 persons (OECD data).

The number of Japanese overseas students decreased from 82,945 in 2004 to 75,156 in 2007, the fall in the number of students going to the US being particularly notable. While the number exceeded 45,000 during the 1990s, it continued to fall, partly due to the aftermath of the 9/11 terrorist attacks, to 29,264 in 2008. By contrast, the number of Indian students going to the US increased to 103,260 in the last decade, three times as many as Japanese students, and the numbers of Chinese and Korean students increased to 99,235 and 75,065 respectively, approximately twice as many as Japanese students (NHK News Commentators Division July, 2010[2]).

The president of Harvard University visited Japan in March 2010 and lamented that the university had only five Japanese undergraduate students in 2009/10, with only one in the first year (*Yomiuri Shimbun*, March 11, 2010 and *Nihon Keizai Shimbun*, March 15, 2010). The number of Japanese students, both undergraduate and graduate, at Harvard University decreased from 151 in 1999/00 to 101 in 2009/10, a drop of about 30% in ten years. This figure contrasts starkly with a rapid increase in the number of Chinese students over the same period from 227 to 463, and the number of Korean students from 183 to 314 (*Yomiuri Shimbun*, March 11, 2010).

According to the aforementioned White Paper, a comparison of the 2004 and 2007 surveys of new recruits at Japanese corporations about overseas posting shows that the number of new employees who 'do not wish to work overseas' increased from 28.7% to 36.2%, and the number of those who would be 'willing to accept overseas posting' decreased from 37.1% to 29.3%. Those who would 'decline overseas posting as long as possible' increased by almost 9% from 21.8% to 30.5%. Further, the percentage of young people in their twenties who leave Japan decreased by almost five points from 24.1% in 1997 to 19.4% in 2007 (Keizai sangyō shō 2010: 286). Thus, both the minds and actions of the youth in general are becoming more inward looking.

After the publication of *Hoshigaranai wakamono tachi* (The young who want nothing) by Taku Yamaoka (2009) of the Research Institute of Industry and Regional Economy, the term *satori sedai* (resigned, or impassive generation) became an Internet buzz-word. For young people, especially young men, turning away from motor cars, drinking and leisure activities were mentioned as symptoms of their orientation towards stability and a lack of propensity to consume. In January 2010 I asked students to examine why Japan's young people were not interested in social activism as the topic for an assignment for my sociology seminar. A female student, who professes to be a member of *satori sedai* herself, wrote as follows: 'We only know the world of post-bubble economic recession. We will *not be able to survive unless we measure our own worth as early as possible and face reality in order to protect our future. Satori sedai* refers to the young who are resigned to a challenging life and try to lead a modest life accordingly. Why would these *young people who do not seek challenges or changes and try to keep their expectations realistic engage themselves in social activism?*' (emphasis added).

Young people who only know bad economic times are risk averse and are thus strongly oriented towards stability. In the World Value Survey, the proportion of Japanese people who thought they did not fall into the category of 'adventure and risk seekers' exceeded 70%, the highest among 48 major countries (Yamagishi and Brinton 2010: 22). In my own experience, this attitude is quite a contrast to the strong motivation for study and life found among overseas students from China, Korea, and Indonesia. There appears to be no way that these Japanese youths can inject dynamism into Japanese society.

More immigrants?

If we cannot expect our politicians or young people to increase social diversity, what else can we turn to? The first potential solution is to change our immigration policy to increase the immigration intake.

According to the estimates of the Ministry of Health, Labor and Welfare, there are about 930,000 foreign workers in Japan, about 760,000 of whom are legal and about 170,000 are illegal. Nearly one million foreign workers are already living in Japan, including those from China and Brazilians of Japanese descent. They are concentrated in metropolitan areas and certain cities with automotive and machine assembly industries such as Hamamatsu in Shizuoka Prefecture and Ōta in Gunma Prefecture. However, it is highly questionable as to whether a national consensus can be reached regarding the liberalization of immigration at a time of excess labor supply and a deepening youth unemployment problem.

The EU and other developed countries are all confronted by the difficult questions of whether to increase immigration or not, what rights should be given to legal and illegal immigrants, and what immigration policy should be adopted. These questions raise concerns about issues such as conflicting economic interests and friction between different cultures.

Reaction to President Obama's call for unity[3]

Paradoxically, racial and religious rifts are widening, especially focusing on Islam, under President Obama, who emphasized that its patchwork heritage was the US's strength and called for a united rather than divided nation. The state governor and the city mayor of New York, both of whom are Democrats, approved the construction plan for a thirteen-story Islamic center and mosque near Ground Zero of the 9/11 terrorist attacks. However, opposing the plan was the group 9/11 Families for a Safe and Strong America as well as Republicans. In the summer of 2010, the controversy developed into nationwide campaigns for and against the construction project. The opinion that the construction should be allowed on the basis of religious freedom clashed with the view that it should not be built near Ground Zero where nearly 3,000 people fell victim to terror attacks engineered by Al Qaeda.

As a backlash against the construction plan, the pastor of a Christian church in Florida proposed that people burn copies of the Koran. President Obama criticized this suggestion and UN Secretary-General Ban Ki-moon appealed to abort the Koran-burning. The governments of Indonesia, Afghanistan, and Pakistan condemned the proposal, and people marched in protest all over the world.

Although President Obama is a Protestant Christian, a CNN opinion survey has found that one in four Americans believes that he is a Muslim. It has been pointed out that the nationwide emergence of the Tea Party Movement from 2009, mainly comprising of conservative Christian right-wing white people, is backed by resentment toward a marked increase in the number of minorities in government posts under an African-American president. In fact, the US has seen a rise in the occurrence of religious hate crimes targeting Muslims and ethnic hate crimes targeting African Americans and Hispanics during 2010, and the number of hate groups claiming to be patriots has increased from 149 in 2008 to 512 in 2009.

Limited social and political participation of women

Japan is lagging far behind the rest of the world in terms of women's social and political participation. In addition to arguments about relative ethnic homogeneity, Japanese society's lack of diversity is clearly demonstrated through the social status of women and the present state of their participation in social and political arenas.

There are currently three female prefectural governors in Japan (Harumi Takahashi of Hokkaidō, Yukiko Kada of Shiga, and Mieko Yoshimura of Yamagata). Fusae Ōta of Osaka (took office in 2000) was the first of six female governors so far. There were 18 female city mayors as of the end of November 2010 (Japan Association of

City Mayors' data), but only two are in ordinance-designated major cities—in Sendai and Yokohama (both took office in August 2009). There have only been two female political party leaders—former Socialist Party leader Takako Doi and current Social Democratic Party leader Mizuho Fukushima.

Fifty-four women were elected to the Lower House in September 2009, occupying 11.3% of the total 480 seats. This was the first time that the ratio of female Lower House members exceeded 10%. Among the 185 countries in the Inter-Parliamentary Union, Japan's ratio of female Lower House members ranks it at 97th place. The ratio is generally high in northern European countries such as Sweden, (ranks 2nd, 47%), Finland (7th, 42%), the Netherlands (8th, 41%) and Denmark (9th, 38%). Japan ranks lower than other major Asian countries such as Vietnam (35th, 26%), China (51st, 21%), the Philippines (54th, 21%), Indonesia (64th, 18%) and Korea (85th, 15%). The number and ratio of female Upper House members in Japan was also low, 44 out of 242 and 17.4%, after the July 2010 election.

The Japanese government proposed that 'efforts should be made in various fields to increase the ratio of women in leadership positions to at least 30% by 2020' in the Basic Plan for Gender Equality (formulated in 2000). As shown in Figure 8.2, however, the only fields that have achieved this goal so far include pharmacists (67.0%), members of national advisory bodies (33.2%), and civil service employees (30.6%). The ratios are still below 20% in professional fields such as lawyers, medical doctors, researchers, journalists, and court judges.

The Gender Empowerment Measure (GEM) released by the United Nations Development Programme (UNDP) is calculated on the basis of the male-female ratio of parliamentary representation, the male-female ratios in professional, technical, and management positions, and differences in estimated income between males and females. It is a leading international indicator of gender equality, and Japan ranks very low among developed countries at 57th out of 109. This is due to Japan's low female representation in the Diet, low representation at the management level, and significant gender-based wage disparity. Since Japan ranked 38th in 1999, its ranking fell 19 places in the last decade and continues to fall. While women's social participation appears on the surface to be increasing in Japan, the rate of increase has been getting slower by international standards.

Japan ranks 10th out of 182 countries when it comes to the Human Development Index (HDI) released by the UNDP which measures the degree of the development of basic human abilities. The HDI is

Figure 8.2: The proportion of women in leadership positions in various fields

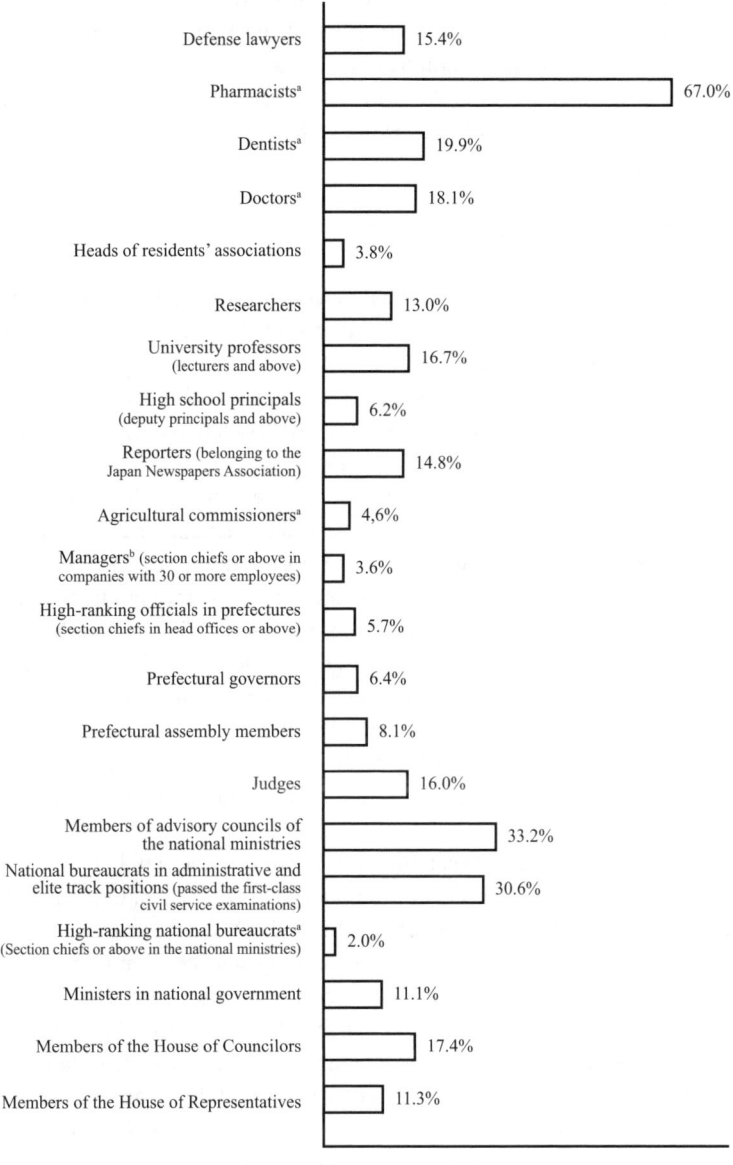

Source: *Josei no seisaku hōshin kettei sankaku jōkyō shirabe* (Survey of the participation levels of women in policy and program making). Data based on information from 2009, except those marked with 'a' (2008) and 'b' (2006).

calculated from various indicators, including life expectancy, years of schooling, adult literacy, and per capita income. The Gender-related Development Index (GDI) is derived by deducting gender difference from each of the indicators of the HDI, and Japan ranks high at 14th out of 155 countries on this scale. Northern European countries such as Sweden, Norway, and Austria tend to rank high for all indices. Japan ranks high for the HDI and the GDI but extremely low for the GEM.

NGOs/NPOs and civil society

Hopes for the development of social diversity now rest on NGOs/NPOs, which have been increasing in number rapidly since legislation was passed in 1998 (Hasegawa 2004, 2005a and 2010). Although Japan had no legal system for affording corporate status to civic action groups for a long time, many NPOs have been organized and are becoming active in various fields. Since the NPO legislation came into operation in December 1998 and the certification system began, the number of certified NPOs exceeded 40,000 by the end of September 2010 (Figure 8.3). This means that an average of 288 corporations were newly certified per month over the last twelve years. The number of public interest corporations (incorporated foundations and associations under Article 34 of the Civil Law Act) was 24,317 as of 1 December 2008, and this figure was surpassed by certified NPOs at the end of November 2005. The fact that the number of certified NPOs overtook that of public interest corporations under the Meiji-era law within seven years of the enactment of the NPO law is indicative of this rapid proliferation of NPOs.

Together with the Internet and mobile phones, the rapid popularization of NPOs counts as one of the major changes in Japanese society during the first decade of the 21st century. Only several years ago, one had to start with an explanation of what NPO signifies, but terms such as *tokutei hi eiri katsudō hōjin* (specified non-profit corporation) and 'NPO' have now taken root in Japanese society. While the National Survey of Life Preferences conducted by the Cabinet Office in January 2000 (Naikaku fu kokumin seikatsu kyoku, 2004) found that nearly half (47.2%) of the respondents had 'no knowledge' of NPOs, the same survey conducted in November 2003 found the ratio of respondents with 'no knowledge' had decreased to 10.5%. Those with 'good knowledge' had increased from 1.7 to 5.9% and those with 'some knowledge' had increased from 19.4 to 44.3% (Figure 8.4). The concept 'not-for-profit,'

Figure 8.3: Number of specified nonprofit organizations (December 1998 to October 2010)

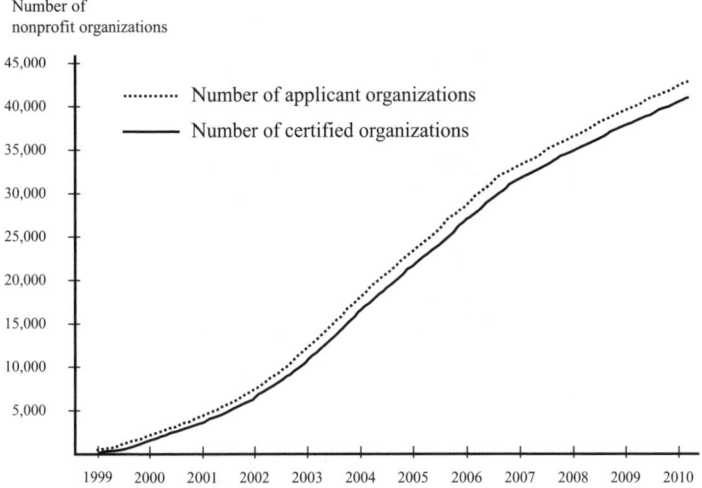

Note: Graph compiled from Cabinet Office data current at the end of October 2010. Data were collected at the end of each month.

where NPO members do not aim to distribute profits among themselves, is rapidly becoming common knowledge among the Japanese.

Table 8.2 shows the categories of NPO activities stated in the articles of incorporation. In Japan, there are 17 specified activity categories (initially 12), and organizations applying for certification must nominate at least one of these categories in their articles of incorporation. The most common categories are health, medical care, and welfare, which are nominated by about 58% of certified NPOs. This is followed by social education and intermediary organizations that seek to improve the abilities and capacities of NPOs. Urban policy, childcare, and nursing are nominated by over 40% of the NPOs. These figures suggest that many of these organizations are involved in the provision of services.

While civil society tends to be mainly seen as a philosophical concept in Japan, in Western society it substantially signifies a complex or network of associations, as argued by Gramsci (1992) or Habermas in the revised preface to his *The Structural Transformation of the Public Sphere* (1989). In fact, NGOs/NPOs are often referred to as 'civil society,' and a moderator may invite 'a comment from the per-

Figure 8.4: Knowledge of NPOs

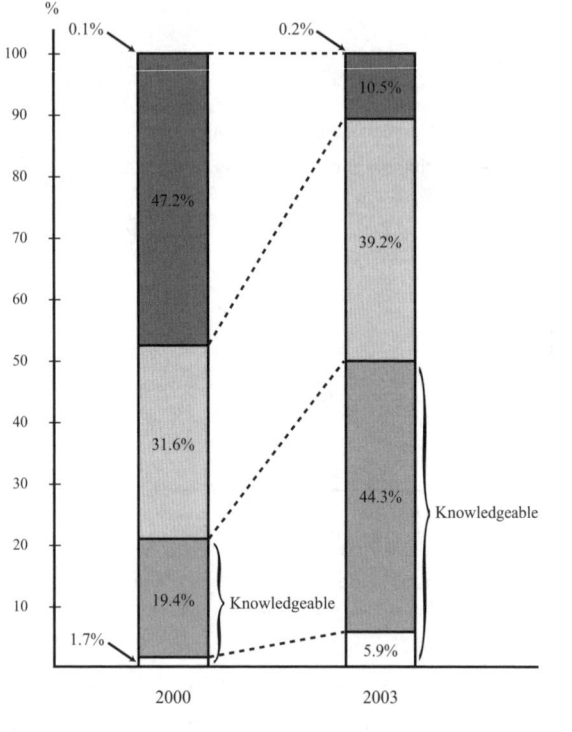

☐ Know fully   ▨ Know to some extent based on newspaper and TV reports   ▪ Do not know at all
▨ Heard the term NPO but do not know what activities these organizations conduct   ▪ No response

Notes:
a. The respondents for 2000 were 3,972 individuals aged between 15 and 69, both male and female, sampled nationwide, and for 2003 there were 3,908 participants aged from 15 to 79. The figure exhibits the patterns of their answers to question 18 in *Kokumin seikatsu senkōdo chōsa* (National survey of life preferences), conducted by the Cabinet Office.
b. Question 18 above in the 2000 survey asked 'In our country, citizens' organizations, including NPOs (non-profit organizations), volunteer organizations which do not seek profits, are active in social welfare and community development. Do you know what kinds of activities NPOs are engaged in? Choose one.'

spective of civil society' at international conferences in opposition to 'government (EU, states, local governments, parliamentarians)' and 'business (corporations)' (Hasegawa, 2005b). The term 'civil society' can be used in reference to NGOs/NPOs individually or collectively. There is a strong feeling that NGOs/NPOs are the real driving forces

Table 8.2: Categories of activities of incorporated NPOs

Categories of activities	Number of incorporated NPOs	Ratio
Health and medical care and welfare	23,625	57.7
Social education	18,973	46.3
Intermediary of organizational management	18,955	46.3
Childcare and nursing	16,991	41.5
Urban policy	16,967	41.4
Academy, culture, arts, and sports	13,688	33.4
Environmental conservation	11,816	28.9
Occupational skills and job opportunities[a]	8,268	20.2
International corporation	7,971	19.5
Human rights and peace	6,504	15.9
Economic activities[a]	5,972	14.0
Community safety	4,178	10.2
Information society[a]	3,718	9.1
Gender relations	3,429	8.4
Disaster relief services	2,603	6.4
Consumer protection[a]	2,423	5.9
Science and technology[a]	2,085	5.1

Note: Tables compiled from Cabinet Office Data current at the end of September 2010. Each organization may appear in multiple acitivity categories. The ratio column indicates the percentage of the total 40,947 corporations engaged in a particular activity at the time. Five categories with 'a' were added when the revised law was enacted on May 1, 2003.

and major players in civil society. Conversely, there are no powerful civil society forces other than NGOs/NPOs.

Let us confirm the definition of NPO here. The most widely accepted definition proposed by Lester Salamon (1992) is as follows. An NPO is:

1. A formal organization, generally having corporate status under state law and the capacity to act as a contracting party;
2. A private organization, independent of the government;
3. A not-for-profit organization that reinvests any profit into its original goal of the public interest;
4. A self-governing organization;
5. An organization of voluntary participants; and
6. An organization serving the public interest.

Non-Governmental Organization (NGO) is another common term often used in contrast with the government in the context of foreign relations and the activities of the United Nations. NPO tends to be used in contrast to business corporations. NGO and NPO are similar in substance.

NPOs in a broad sense in an American context form a very comprehensive, residual category of entities bundled under the 'not-for-profit' banner and approximately 1.4 million organizations are registered. This category includes business associations such as chambers of commerce and industry, trade associations and labor unions whose original purpose is to serve the interest of their members although they serve public interest as well, and foundations and churches. These groups enjoy the privilege of exemption from federal income tax under the Internal Revenue Service (the legal definition of NPO in the US is a category of tax exempt organizations under its taxation law). Unlike in Europe where there are many national and state institutions, many of the orchestras, art galleries, and zoos in the US are NPOs, in addition to the public broadcasting services (PBS) on TV and radio. This broad definition of NPO is almost identical to that of NGO and organizations from the NPO sector. This sector accounted for 5.2% of the US gross domestic product (GDP) as of 2005 (National Center for Charitable Statistics 2007).

An NPO in a narrow sense is a management organization that carries out economic and business activities and is a type of business entity providing public services. While it is not permitted to distribute profit to shareholders or members (therefore consumer cooperatives are not NPOs in the US), it can receive business earnings and pay salaries to its full-time staff. Peter Drucker (1990) and other management experts have proposed theories on NPO management practices.

Of particular importance is that these NPOs enjoy the privilege of discounted postage costs as well as tax deductions on donations under Article 501 (C) (3) of the Internal Revenue Service, in addition to the aforementioned federal income tax exemption. Citizens can financially support and nurture NPOs in a narrow sense according to their own interest and liking.

In comparison with the narrowly defined understanding of NPO, NGO is a broader concept. Labor unions and consumer cooperatives are essentially mutual-aid organizations for the protection of the rights and interests of their members. These organizations, for which public service is not a primary purpose, can be regarded as NGOs but not as NPOs.

A crucial event prompting the need for a legal system that would give corporate status to civic organizations in Japan was the Great Hanshin Earthquake of January 1995. However, since the beginning of the 1990s the need for such a system had been noticed in a number of fields, including aged care, environmental policy, and foreign aid. Thus it is too simplistic to overstate the role of the Great Hanshin Earthquake in this situation (Hasegawa, Shinohara, and Broadbent 2007).

The Act on the Promotion of Specified Non-Profit Activities (the 1998 NPO Act enacted on March 25, 1998) provides a legal system by which an organization of ten or more members with at least three directors and one auditor/supervisor among them can easily obtain corporate status. No basic establishment fund is required, and there is no minimum membership fee revenue.

Previously, incorporated foundations were generally required to have around 300 million yen in basic funds, and in many cases this requirement prevented ordinary civic organizations from gaining corporate status. Incorporated associations were required to have a stable annual membership revenue of about ten million yen. There was also a system of 'approval' for both incorporated foundations and associations by the competent authorities (in the case of nationwide activity) or the prefectural government. Government officials wielded great discretionary powers over the approval process, and it was virtually impossible for foundations opposing government policies to obtain approval.

The great importance of the NPO Act lies in the simple fact that there are no basic funding or membership revenue requirements and applicants are basically 'certified' by the prefectural government (or the cabinet office if they have offices in more than one prefecture). Government authorities cannot arbitrarily become involved in this process.

Article 1 of the NPO Act states that its purpose is 'to promote the sound development of specified nonprofit activities in the form of volunteer and other activities freely performed by citizens to benefit society and thereby to contribute to the advancement of the public interest.' This is the only Japanese law that uses the word 'citizen,' highlighting the extent to which the Japanese government has shunned the word.

The NPO Act was a member's bill submitted by members of the ruling coalition of the LDP, the Social Democratic Party (SDP), and the New Party Sakigake in December 1996 (although the SDP and

Sakigake were non-cabinet allies from November 1996) which was passed in March 1998 and put into operation in December 1998. It was a product of an unprecedented period of coalition between the LDP, the SDP, and Sakigake, lasting from June 1994 to November 1996. It is notable that the institutionalization of NPOs took place rapidly in the mid-1990s on the back of post-Cold War globalization, not only in Japan but also in the rest of the world. As discussed below, NPOs/NGOs became active in East Asia as well.

About 80% of Korea's NGOs were organized after the democratization of the country in 1987, especially after the period of President Kim Young-sam (1993–1996) (Kim and McNeal 2005). Many environmental movements were also organized after the Rio Summit in 1992 (Ku 2001). In China, NGO activities gained momentum after the 1995 World Conference on Women in Beijing and the Severe Acute Respiratory Syndrome (SARS) pandemic in 2003. Li Yanyan (in press) has conducted a comparative study of similarities and differences between Japanese and Chinese NPOs. China has adopted the NGO concept, implementing Regulations on the Administration of Social Organizations (revised in 1989) and Regulations on the Registration and Administration of Social Organizations (revised in 1998), which are equivalent to Japan's NPO Act. They facilitate a process to provide corporate status and registration for social organizations. Li adopts a comprehensive view of NGOs and counts registered social organizations, non-commercial private organization, foundations, grassroot NGOs, and neighborhood organizations as types of NGOs.

Significance of NGO/NPO activities

What is the social significance of NPOs and what roles can they play in society? First, NPOs complement the roles played by the market and the government. NPOs can supply public goods and collective consumption goods that are unavailable due to 'market failure' and 'government failure,' with self-help, participation, voluntarism, and the necessity principle as keywords, without being constrained by precedent, within the extent of their capabilities, and in a flexible manner. They play a significant role especially in the fields of welfare, medical care, environment, and education.

Second, in relation to social and civic movements, NPOs are an institutionalized or organized form of such movements. Although not all NPOs are social movement organizations, many of these entities that carry out organized and sustained activities take the form of

NPOs in contemporary Japan. In the US and Europe, social movement organizations tend to have a permanent office with full-time staff, employ lawyers and economic analysts, recruit members, and invite donations in order to increase their influence. Social movements show their presence by exerting their social influence, especially on the policy-making process, and gain support from the media and the public which in turn enable them to grow further.

'Resource mobilization theory' is a leading social movement theory espousing the view that there is no fundamental difference between the development process of a management organization and that of a social movement/campaign organization, and that the effective mobilization of people, goods, money, and symbols through the adoption of clear strategies and tactics hold the key to the successful development of a movement. It emerged in the mid-1970s based on the experiences of the civil rights movement and student activism of the 1960s in the US, and subsequently became the mainstream approach internationally. The present state of NPOs is a good example of the application of resource mobilization theory.

Third, NPOs are receptacles for civic and volunteer activities and serve as the center of a network that stocks human resources, information, and funds. Many local residents' campaigns have been initiated across Japan since the mid-1960s, but they were mostly single-issue movements and usually followed a pattern in which they were formed in response to emerging concerns in local communities, lost momentum once the problems were solved, then became dormant or dissolved. The continuation of activities has been a problem for residents' movements across the board, and the absence of an effective solution has meant that it has been difficult to accumulate and pass on experience and knowledge. Becoming an NPO with corporate status, assets, and business activity means gaining an institutional framework to inherit or pass on activities and campaigns.

Major US cities have NPO directories. There are citizens' networks independent of businesses and governments which advise citizens with problems who to turn to in order to gain useful information or access services. Some Japanese cities with thriving civic activities have NPO activity support centers that are good sources of local NPO information. In Miyagi Prefecture, for example, citizens' activity support centers are found in Natori, Iwanuma, and Tagajō as well as Sendai.

Fourth, NPOs can act as social watchdog agencies that monitor and counteract the activities of big businesses and governments. J. K. Galbraith (1952) termed the ability to offset the market power of private enterprises 'countervailing power,' and NPOs have this form of presence in contemporary America.

Through the establishment of organizational foundations and the accumulation of human resources, funds, information-gathering capacity, and policy-analysis and planning capacity, Japanese NPOs are becoming the leading social watchdog agencies that act as a countervailing force to replace declining labor unions. Representatives of NPOs and NGOs are joining advisory committees of the central and local governments in increasing numbers.

Fifth, NPOs are the important driving forces behind social diversity and plurality. In Japan, human resources have a low level of mobility. Businesses and government agencies tend to hold on to their personnel, and labor unions are fundamentally company-based workers unions. It has been difficult for some citizens' movements to secure competent full-time staff due to the low wages attached to the positions. By contrast, working as full-time employees at prominent environmental organizations is in itself a career-building step in the US and England, and job applications come pouring in when staff vacancies at leading NPOs are advertised. NPOs attract motivated and capable people.

Networking through frequent exchange of personnel between NPOs, government agencies, businesses, and universities is a source of creativity, dynamism, and vitality in the US and Europe. For example, it is not uncommon for employees in charge of environmental affairs at business corporations to go independent after a certain period and set up their own environmental consultancy business or NPO. NPOs have injected some fresh air into the business sectors and bureaucracies of the US and Europe and beyond.

Sixth, small-scale, 'grassroots' NPOs often have their bases in the local community and therefore can play an important role in increasing the vitality, self-government, and diversity of the local community. In Japan, NPOs have been conducting their activities in relatively wide areas such as an entire prefecture or city or several municipalities. In the future, NPOs are expected to replace neighborhood associations and other local residents' organizations, which are suffering from the adverse effects of aging and fixed leadership, to support the vitality of local communities such as elementary school districts.

Challenges for NPOs

NPOs are of course also facing serious organizational challenges. Salamon proposes the concept of 'voluntary failure' in reference to 'government failure' and 'market failure' (1995: 44–48). This involves a general lack of necessary resources, demand–supply gaps preventing resources from reaching where they are truly needed, philanthropic paternalism, and philanthropic amateurism which tends to favor non-expert opinions even when expert views are needed. NPOs are prone to remain inefficient for the very reason that their organization is based on voluntarism, spontaneity, and a sense of mission for public interests, and due to the fact that it is difficult to measure their performance, as discussed below.

The effect of specialization and institutionalization can be a double-edged sword for NPOs. Increased specialization can widen the psychological distance between the leadership group and the general membership, turning many members into passive participants who simply pay their fees and receive newsletters. Institutionalization such as the establishment of NPO-related legislative frameworks is indispensable for the development of stable organizational foundations, but it tends to hamper their ability to generate voluntary and spontaneous energy for their movement.

The Iron Law of Oligarchy, theorized by Robert Michels (1911), is applicable to NPOs as well. This idea was originally developed based on a case study of political parties and was then expanded to organizations in general. It posits that organizational growth inevitably leads to centralization, bureaucratization, and minority control. In NPOs, board members are often unpaid and work part-time and tend to rely heavily on the salaried full-time staff at the secretariat. The phenomenon of a board of directors in name only and a secretariat in a *de facto* leadership position is also often found in public utility corporations.

It is a common occurrence abroad that giant NGOs that are well known and media-savvy such as Greenpeace end up dragging along long-term, low-profile local grassroots NGOs. A campaign by a giant NGO has the capacity to suddenly ignite social controversy, but it can also have a negative impact on long-term grassroots movements when media attention and social interest wane once the NGO moves on to other issues.

The ascertaining of NPO membership itself is a difficult problem in the first place. While those who are registered as members and pay membership fees are basically members in the case of a membership organization, many NPOs in the welfare sector treat recipients of their services as members. In some cases, secretariat officers who exert a strong influence over the operation of NPOs are not actual members. In the case of NPOs, there is more than one definition of membership and formal membership rules often do not reflect the actual state of organizational operation. However, the difficulty of ascertaining membership numbers is a sign of NPO's diversity and flexibility.

It is difficult to make objective evaluations of NPOs. The performance of a profit-making organization can be evaluated in terms of the market, i.e., customers, consumers, clients, and the stock market. This evaluation is converted into management indicators such as sales and finance and must be audited by law. If a commercial enterprise fails to raise funds, it cannot procure raw materials and hence cannot provide further goods and services. In the case of an NPO, however, a qualitative evaluation on the level of accomplishment of its mission is important. Numerical indicators such as budget, balance sheet, membership size, and membership revenue alone are not sufficient for making a qualitative evaluation. It is not easy to survey or measure the level of satisfaction among members of an NPO either. Of course, qualitative evaluations such as corporate social responsibility (CSR) measures are also difficult in the case of profit-making organizations.

One concern regarding Japanese NPOs is the risk of their degeneration into cheap subcontractors to government agencies. Yayoi Tanaka (2006) has conducted a detailed analysis of the actual state of subcontractorization. In fact, there are many NPOs, especially in regional areas, that have been substantially arranged and supported by government agencies. NPOs have virtually become the subcontractors of government agencies in many cases, particularly in the fields of aged care, community beautification projects, and town planning and facility management. Some joke that NPO must be an acronym for New Partnership Organization. If a government agency employs a university graduate for 38 years until his or her retirement at an annual salary of about eight million yen, it will amount to a labor cost of about 300 million yen on a lifetime wage basis. If the same agency subcontracts an NPO on an annual contract basis, it may be able to reduce the labor cost down to about two million yen per person per year if a motivated and interested citizen is employed at an hourly rate of 800 yen for eight hours a day for twenty-five days per month.

In order to nurture NPOs while curtailing these harmful effects, the role of the intermediaries of organizational management is important. These intermediaries perform functions such as allocating personnel appropriately, providing information and resources to NPOs, mediating between NPO activities and the needs of the community, providing support and assistance to NPOs for training, consultation and advice, networking between NPOs, and conducting surveys on local and international NPO activities and public attitudes.

Notes

Chapter One

1. Here I use data from the Japanese National Census (Statistical Bureau, Management and Coordination Agency, Japan 1967, 1972, 1977, 1982, 1987, 1991, 1996; Statistical Bureau, Ministry of Public Management, Home Affairs, Posts and Telecommunications, Japan 2001; Statistical Bureau, Ministry of Internal Affairs and Communications, Japan 2006). This is because the Census is the most reliable source for the proportion of unmarried women. I concentrate on data on women aged 25 to 34, because most Japanese women enter into their first marriage in this age range.
2. This model was showcased in *AGORA*, the joint Newsletter of the Research Committee on Rational Choice of the International Sociological Association and Section on Rationality and Society of the American Sociological Association, vol. 9, no. 2, 2001.
3. Here I pay particular attention to regular/full-time employment (in non-agricultural sectors). Strictly speaking, full-time employment is not exactly the same as regular employment and vice versa. However, many social scientists point out that the overlap between or intersection of full-time and permanent part-time employment is broad in Japanese society, although, in some cases, casual or irregular employees work as if they are full-time or regular employees with respect to working hours and/or job description (cf. Stockman, Bonney, and Xuewen 1995: 95–96).
4. The Basic Survey of Wage Structure reports the wage distribution for 'standard employees,' who are employed by enterprises immediately after graduating from school or university and have been working for them ever since. In this sense, 'standard employees' represent only a sector of regular employees. However, I use the Basic Survey of Wage Structure as this is the most reliable source of information on individual wage distribution in Japan.
5. 'Wage' and 'income' are not interchangeable in English. However, the Basic Survey on Wage Structure does distinguish between wage and salary. Moreover, wage or salary is the main source of income for most employees in Japan. Thus, I use the words 'wage' and 'income' interchangeably in this chapter.
6. Although Kimura's (2000) model concerns lifetime income, the tests in this chapter utilize the monthly wage or income. This may yield biased estimations of the median and the standard deviation.
7. For simplicity, I postulate here that a man and a woman of the same age group would likely marry.
8. In Japan, wages for part-time workers are usually lower than those for full-time workers even if the substance of the work is the same. Moreover, there have been some rules that have suppressed the working hours of part-time workers, such as the spousal deduction (*haigūsha kōjo*) in the Japanese tax

system and the third insured person (*dai 3-gō hihokensha*) in the Japanese National Pension scheme.

Chapter Two

1. According to the OECD Family database, the rate of poverty in single parent households in Japan (in the mid-2000s) was 58.7%, the highest among the 30 OECD nations. The average for the thirty nations was 30.8%, and among major nations the US was 47.5%, Germany 41.5%, the UK 23.7%, France 19.3%, and Sweden 7.9%. The criterion for the poverty line is set at less than 50% of the median income of the total population (OECD 2010).
2. This chapter looks at five nations: Sweden, Germany, France, the UK, and the US, because in international comparisons Japan's social security and social welfare systems are typically compared to those of these five countries. For example, in its international comparison of The Cost of Social Security in Japan, the National Institute of Population and Social Security Research publishes an annual comparison of Japan and these nations.
3. The proportion of divorces by arbitration and those by court case in which there is a determination regarding paternal payment of child support where the mother is appointed guardian. Figures from the Supreme Court General Secretariat (2009).
4. The information on the systems in the five countries is from Corden (1999) and Skinner et al. (2007). In this chapter mothers are explained to be the custodial parent and fathers the non-custodial parent, but the situation is the same in the reversed instance.

Chapter Three

1. A nationwide collection of cases commended for good deeds compiled and published by the Tokugawa shogunate in 1801. The edition used here is Sugano, Noriko (ed.) (1999).
2. See Matsuzaki (2007, 2008) for detailed analysis covering the medieval–early modern transition period to the middle of the early modern period.
3. A family tree passed on in the Shimazu family. The edition used here is Shōko Shūseikan (The museum of the Shimazu family) (ed.) (1985).
4. A compendium of genealogies of *daimyōs* and retainers compiled by the Tokugawa shogunate from 1799 to 1812. The edition used here is Takayanagi, Mitsutoshi, Taishi Okayama, and Kazuma Saiki (eds.) (1964).
5. A collection of materials compiled by Satsuma historians Sueyoshi and Suemichi Ijichi from the late early modern period to the Meiji period. The edition used here is Kagoshima Ken Ishin Shiryō Hensanjo (Kagoshima Prefectural Historiographical Institute of the Meiji Restoration) (ed.) (1971–1978).
6. Materials used here are taken from Tokyo Daigaku Shiryō Hensanjo (Historiographical Institute, The University of Tokyo) (ed.) (1942–1966).
7. *Kankoku kōgi roku* (see Note 1). Kagoshima Kenritsu Sendai Kōtō Jogakkō Kōyūkai (The Graduates' Association of Kagoshima Prefectural Sendai Girls' High School) (1915): a collection of the stories of dutiful Kagoshima women from the middle of the early modern period to the Meiji period. Kagoshima Jinjō Kōtō Shōgakkō (Kagoshima Higher Elementary School)

(1922): a collection of the stories of dutiful Kogoshima people from the middle of the early modern period to the Meiji period. Kagoshima Ken Kyōiku Chōsa Kai (Kagoshima Prefectural Educational Investigation) (1927): the stories of dutiful people of Ōshima in Kagoshima from the late early modern period to the Meiji period. Kagoshima Ken Aira Gun Kokubu Mura Kyōikukai (The Educational Committee of Kokubun Village, Aira Country, Kagoshima Prefecture) (1917): the deeds of Kinzaemon Nagasaki who was born to a peasant family in 1871.
8. Zaidanhōjin Bunkazai Kenzōbutsu Hozon Gijutsu Kyōkai (The Japanese Association for the Conservation of Architectural Monuments) (1987).
9. Shimazu (1983).
10. The family precepts contained in The Shimazu Press (1978).
11. Kagoshima Ken Joshi Shihan Gakkō (Kagoshima Prefectural Female Teacher's School) (ed.) (1940). A collection of documents about the leading women of the Satsuma domain from the end of the Edo period to the Shōwa period, compiled as a supplementary reader for ethics, Japanese, and history classes in senior years of girls' high school.
12. In complying with the wishes of Teneiin (Hiroko), the 5th Satsuma lord Tsugutoyo Shimazu took Take, the adopted daughter of the 8th Shogun Yoshimune, as his wife. According to Take's dying wishes, Shige, the daughter of the 8th Satsuma lord Shigehide, became the wife of the 11th Shogun Ienari and from this relationship, Atsu, the adopted daughter of the 11th Satsuma lord Nariakira, became the wife of the 13th Shogun Iesada.
13. 'Tanegashima Shōjuin' in Nishimura (1899).
14. Shimazu, Nobuhisa (ed.) (2005). 'Gosaishi teiyō'; (A compendium of ancestral rituals of the Shimazu family): historical material of ancestral rituals passed on in the main Shimazu family containing information about individual ancestors to be worshipped.
15. See Kagoshma Ken Kyōiku Iinkai (Kagoshima Prefectural Educational Investigation Committee) (1975) and Ono (1982). Also, a private house built in Satsuma between 1830 and 1844 was reconstructed and displayed at Reimeikan (Kagoshima Prefectural Center of Historical Materials).
16. The 1916 noble hereditary property law enforcement regulations governing the hereditary property of the nobility provided for the household management council to discuss matters concerning the hereditary property of the nobility. They allowed certain people other than councilors to attend council meetings and voice their opinions. These people included a family head, his parents living at his home, wife, presumptive heir, main and branch families' heads, guardians, guardian-supervisors, and curators. Thus, the mother and the wife of the family head were given a chance to express their opinions. The family precept of the Shimazu family, however, had no such provisions. I would like to consider possible reasons for this exclusion and the diminishment of women's right to be involved in household management in a future study.
17. *Kyōdo Fujin Tokuhon* (see Note 11). See Hanada (1921).
18. Nagano (2003) analyzes the reconstruction of gender in the early Meiji period using the example of a *kabuki* play about Kasuga-no-tsubone who served the shogun's family, but it emphasizes Kasuga-no-tsubone's absolute obedience to her husband as wife rather than her role as mother.

Chapter Four

1. In referring to Koreans in Japan, no single term attained a dominant position; the definition of the terminology is useful. In this chapter, I use the term 'zainichi' to refer to all pre-war Korean immigrants and their descendants (old-comers) living in Japan, regardless of their political affiliation or citizenship status.
2. Since many *zainichi* left in Japan who visited family members that repatriated to North Korea through Booksong Saup found that a large part of the premises provided by Chongryun and North Korea were not true, they became angry and despaired when observing the sufferings of those who returned to their homeland, North Korea (Lee 1999a).
3. North Korea's decision to withdraw from the Nuclear Non-proliferation Treaty and the 2006 testing of a nuclear bomb in an underground facility in North Korea exacerbated the social antagonism against North Korea and Chongryun in Japan (Lee 1999a; Kim 2004).
4. In 1998, the committee for the constructive education of Tokyo Chosun middle and high schools (Tokyo Chosen Chū-Kōkyū Gakko Kensetsu Iinkai) presented a strong request regarding the fundamental reform of the ethnic school system. They objected to the North Korean-style education system and requested that ethnic school education would be made appropriate for preparing their children to live in Japan (Lee 1999a).
5. At the 1999 Convention, a report entitled 'Suggestions for fundamentally changing the nature of its activities to develop Chongryun into a compatriot mass organization truly serving the *zainichi* compatriots as a whole' was presented with the subtitle 'The acuteness of the need for reorientation' (*Choong-ang Ilbo*, October 12, 1999). In the report, it was argued that despite the demographic changes affecting the *zainichi* community, Chongryun activities still 'require only a political ideology based on fixed formality [...] this has given the impression of the rigidity of the organisation' (Jin 2001: 25). It was also emphasized that Chongryun needs to respect the *zainichi* public's perspectives and needs (*Chosun Shinbo*, September 27, 1999).
6. In response to Chongryun's allegations published in *Chosun Shinbo* about him, Hong took out a lawsuit with a large numbers of supporters and won his case in September 2006.

Chapter Five

1. Prior to the movement of the 1970s, campaigns were launched to denounce the US government for the mistreatment of Japanese Americans (Murray 1995; Maki et al. 1999). Due to its focus, this chapter only refers to the movement of the 1970s. For discussion of the political and legislative process behind the movement, see Hatamiya (1993) and Maki et al. (1999).
2. Under suspicion of being in conspiracy with the Japanese empire that was an enemy to the US, Japanese Americans residing in the Pacific coastal areas and areas of Hawaii were forcibly relocated to camps from 1942 to 1946.
3. The term 'reparation' here manifests in many forms, such as a public

acknowledgement and apology, monetary compensation, return of goods, and restoration of ruined facilities.
4. In general, the three groups, the Japanese American Citizens (JACL), the National Coalition for Japanese American Redress (NCJAR) and NCRR took leadership roles in the Japanese American movement. Although their goals were common in pursuing redress and reparation from the US government, their approaches differed. The founding members and leaders of JACL and NCJAR consisted of members of the second generation of Japanese Americans who experienced internment during the Second World War.
5. The interviews with Kimoto took place on March 31, August 7, and August 11 in 2004, on August 16 and December 18, 2005, on September 17, 2006, and on February 27 and March 5, 2008. In the quotations, each bracket [] indicates supplementary explanations made by the author.
6. Immediately after the Pearl Harbor attack, the FBI arrested and removed the leaders and influential members of the Japanese American community, based on a prepared list (Commission on Wartime Relocation and Internment of Civilians (CWRIC) 1997: 54–55).
7. Based on an interview with Nick Araki conducted on April 17, 2004, one of NCRR's founding members.
8. Based on an interview with Max Arita conducted on April 7, one of NCRR's founding members.
9. Based on an interview with Nick Araki conducted on August 17, 2004.
10. Italicized by the author.
11. Influenced by the Asian American women's movement, when Kimoto and her fellow young Japanese Americans founded NCRR, they attempted to maintain gender equality in their organizational structure by establishing a co-chair system. The co-chairs were comprised of one male and one female member.
12. This quote is taken from an interview with Nick Araki conducted on August 17, 2004.

Chapter Six

1. Even the BBC, which makes a point of neutrality, reported that a Muslim organization protested against the Iraq War by holding up placards saying 'Anglican Soldiers Go To Hell,' without explaining the context and background of the protest (*BBC News At Ten*, 3 August, 2009). Such a description of Muslims is dangerous as it feeds the biased view against this group.
2. On the relationship between social recognition and identity, refer to Taylor (1991).
3. Nissa Finney and Ludi Simpson (2009) identified issues with the data sampling method employed by YouGov. YouGov adopts a method of self-selected panels, which is not a standard sample design. They thus warn that '(o)ne should be especially suspicious of' the results reported by YouGov (2009: 96–7).
4. According to a report by the BBC itself, large numbers of people gathered around the BBC building to protest against the appearance of Griffin on *Question Time*. The resistance was intense and a protestor shouting 'BBC!

Shame on you!' was routed out of the building by guards (*BBC News At Ten*, 22 October, 2009).
5. This quiz game is called 'Who's British?' Teachers and volunteers show pupils figures with captions; for example, 'I was born here, though my mum and dad were both born in Sylhet in Bangladesh. I support England in football. But you can't really support them for cricket, can you?' Then, they ask pupils, 'who's British?' Almost all of the correct answers to the questions are 'British.' This quiz has the effect of destroying pupils' stereotypes about standard British identity represented by White English.
6. I gathered information on the global citizenship program from the community organization that ran the program in collaboration with Y school.
7. The effect of the Internet is in fact ambivalent. The Internet, on the one hand, provides opportunities for people to interact with different cultures. However, on the other hand, it also has the potential to strengthen people's conservative traditional values and, at worst, promulgate radical and dangerous ideas. Lewis explains that some young Muslims have been influenced by ancient Islamic texts containing reactionary materials that are now available in English for the young online (Lewis 2007: 45–6).

Chapter Seven

1. This study was supported by KAKENHI (15730283, 18730381). This chapter is a revised version of Tsujimoto, Kuniyoshi, and Yokuda (2007) and Tsujimoto (2008), both published in Japanese.
2. Based on the results of analysis by evolutionary simulation, Koike, Nakamaru, and Tsujimoto (2010) argue that, in addition to peer selection, ROSCAs should introduce a rule forbidding members from receiving funds if they fail to pay their contributions before receiving funds.
3. All the names of the subjects are anonymous to protect their privacy.
4. In order to discuss this point in detail, an explanation about the workings of the bidding method would be required. However, this discussion is omitted from this chapter since the bidding method is complex and entails various forms. Tsujimoto (2000) explains the workings of the bidding method in detail. Besley, Coate, and Loury (1993) include a detailed comparison of random allocation and the bidding method in their analysis of the ROSCA system using mathematical modeling.

Chapter Eight

1. Jōmon culture refers to the culture of the Jōmon period, Japan's prehistoric period from about 14,000 to 300 BCE. The name 'Jōmon' is based on *Jōmon* (cord-patterned) styled earthenware. Jōmon people were hunter-gatherers.
2. See, http://www.nhk.or.jp/kaisetsu-blog/100/54780.html retrieved November 30, 2010.
3. This section draws heavily on Kazuyoshi Takagi (2010).

Bibliography

Ahmed, Sughra (2009), *Seen and Not Heard: Voices of Young British Muslims*, Leicestershire: Policy Research Centre.
Aitchson, John, and James A. C. Brown (1957), *The Lognormal Distribution: With Special Reference to Its Uses in Economics*, Cambridge: Cambridge University Press.
Akasaka, Norio (2007), *Okamoto Taro ga mita Nihon* (New image of Japan from Tarō, Okamoto), Tokyo: Iwanami shoten.
Alam, M. Yunis (2002), *Kilo*, Glasshoughton: Route.
Alam, M. Yunis (2006), *Made in Bradford*, Pontefract: Route.
Ameli, Saied Reza, (2002), *Globalization, Americanization and British Identity*, London: Islamic College for Advanced Studies Press.
Amino, Yoshihiko (2000), *Nippon towa nanika* (What is so-called Japan?), Tokyo: Kōdan-sha.
Aoki, Michio (2008), 'Ninjōbon ni miru Edo shomin josei no dokusho to kyōyō: Tamenaga Shunsui "Umegoyomi" shirīzu wo sozai ni,' (Reading and culture of commoner women in Edo: Analysis of Ninjō-bon 'Umegoyomi' series by Shunsui Tamenaga, *Rekishi hyōron* (Historical review), 694: 25–38.
Ardener, Shirley (1964), 'The comparative study of rotating credit associations,' *Journal of the Royal Anthropological Institute of Great Britain and Ireland*, 94: 201–229.
Ardener, Shirley and Sandra Burman (eds.) (1995), *Money-Go-Rounds: The Importance of Rotating Savings and Credit Associations for Women*, Oxford: Berg.
Baringhorst, Sigrid (1992), 'Cultural pluralism and anti-discrimination policy,' in Dietrich Thränhardt (ed.), *Europe, A New Immigration Continent: Policies and Politics in Comparative Perspective*, Münster: Lit Verlag, 177–97.
Beck, Ulrich (1986), *Risk Society: Towards a New Modernity*, London: SAGE Publications.
Becker, Gary S. (1991[1964]), *A Treatise on the Family*, enlarged edition, Cambridge: Harvard University Press.
Bergman, Helena and Barbara Hobson (2002), 'Compulsory fatherhood: The case of fatherhood in the Swedish welfare state,' in Barbara Hobson (ed.), *Making Men into Fathers: Men, Masculinities, and the Social Politics of Fatherhood*, Cambridge: Cambridge University Press, 92–123.
Besley, Timothy, Stephen Coate, and Glenn Loury (1993), 'The economics of rotating savings and credit associations,' *American Economic Review*, 83: 792–810.
Blair, Tony (2006), 'The duty of integration: Shared British values.' Retrievied August 1, 2009, http://www.number10.gov.uk/Pag e10563.
Brooks, Roy L. (1999), 'The age of apology,' Roy L. Brooks (ed.), *When Sorry isn't Enough: The Controversy over Apologies and Reparations for Human Injustice*, New York: New York University Press, 3–11.

Brooks, Roy L. (2003), 'Reflections on reparations,' in John Torpey, (ed.), *Politics and the Past: On Repairing Historical Injustices*, Lanham: Rowman & Littlefield Publishers, 103–114.

Burlet, Stacey and Helen Reid (1998), 'A gendered uprising: Political representation and minorities,' *Ethnic and Racial Studies*, 21(2): 270–87.

Cairns, Alan (2003), 'Coming to terms with the past,' in John Torpey (ed.), *Politics and the Past: On Repairing Historical Injustices*, Lanham: Rowman & Littlefield Publishers, 63–90.

Campaign Against Racism and Fascism (2001), 'The summer of rebellion: Special report,' *IRR News*, August 1, 2001. Retrieved August 30, 2007 http://www.irr.org.uk/2001/august/ak000001.html

Choong-ang Ilbo, October 12, 1999.

Chosun Shinbo, September 27, 1999.

Chung, Chinsung (2005), 'Chochongryun jojik yungu' (Study on Chongryun), *International and Regional Studies*, 14(4): 33–62.

Commission on Integration and Cohesion (2007), *Shared Our Future*, Wetherby: Commission on Integration and Cohesion.

Commission on Wartime Relocation and Internment of Civilians (1997), *Personal Justice Denied*, San Francisco: The Civil Liberties Public Education Fund.

Communities and Local Government (2009), *Citizenship Survey: 2008–09*, London: Department for Communities and Local Government.

Corden, Anne (1999), *Making Child Maintenance Regimes Work*, London: Family Studies Centre.

Coventry City Council (1986), *Coventry Trends: A Statistical Digest of Ethnic Minority Population*, Coventry: City of Coventry.

Crosby, Faye, J. (1982), *Relative Deprivation and Working Women*, New York: Oxford University Press.

Department for Education and Science (1985), *Education for All: Final Report of the Committee of Inquiry into the Education of Children from Ethnic Minority Groups*, London: HMSO.

Drucker, Peter (1990), *Managing the Non-profit Organisation*, Woburn: Butterworth-Heinemann.

Dwyer, Claire and Bindi Shah (2009), 'Rethinking the identities of young British Muslim women: Educational experiences and aspirations,' in Peter Hopkins and Richard Gale (eds.) *Muslims in Britain: Race, Place and Identities*, Edinburgh: Edinburgh University Press, 55–73.

Ego, Michiko (1998), 'Buke no Edo yashiki no seikatsu II: Kagoshima han Shimazu ke nakaoku nikki kara' (Lifestyle at a samurai residence in Edo II: According to the journal of the nakaoku of the Shimazu family of Kagoshima domain),' *Minato Kuritsu Minato Kyōdo Shiryōkan, Kenkyū kiyō* (Research bulletin of the Minato City Local History Museum), 5: 24.

Finney, Nissa and Ludi Simpson (2009), *Sleepwalking to Segregation?*, Bristol: The Policy Press.

Frey, Bruno S. and Reiner Eichenberger (1996), 'Marriage paradoxes,' *Rationality and Society*, 8(2): 187–206.

Fukuda, Chizuru (2005), 'Kinsei chūki ni okeru Hikone Iike no okumuki' (*Oku* of the Ii family in the Hikone domain in the middle of the Edo period), *Hikonejō hakubutsukan sōsho 6: Buke no seikatsu to kyōyō* (Library of Hikone Castle

Museum 6: Life and culture of the samurai family), Hikone: Hikone Castle Museum, 90–111.

Gaertner, Samuel, L. and John F. Dovidio (2000), *Reducing Intergroup Bias: The Common Ingroup Identity Model*, Philadelphia: Psychology Press.

Galbraith, John K. (1952), *American Capitalism: The Concept of Countervailing Power*, Boston: Houghton Mifflin.

Geertz, Clifford (1962), 'The rotating credit association: A "middle rung" in development,' *Economic Development and Cultural Change*, 10: 241–263.

Gibrat, Robert (1931), *Les inégalités économiques*, Paris: Sirey.

Giddens, Anthony (1991), *Modernity and Self-Identity: Self and Society in the Modern Age*, Oxford: Blackwell Publishing.

Giddens, Anthony (1994), 'Living in a post-traditional society,' in Ulrich Beck, Anthony Giddens and Scott Lash (eds.), *Reflexive Modernization: Politics, Tradition and Aesthetics in the Modern Social Order*, Cambridge: Polity Press, 56–109.

Gramsci, Antonio (1992), *Prison Notebooks*, Joseph A. Buttigieg (ed.), Joseph A. Buttigieg and Antonio Callari (translators), New York: Columbia University Press.

Habermas, Ürgen (1989), *The Structural Transformation of the Public Sphere: An inquiry into a category of bourgeois society*, Thomas Burger (translator), Cambridge: MIT press.

Hanada, Nakanosuke (1921), *Hōtoku shūyoū kunwa* (A collection of lectures by Nakanosuke Hanada from Kagoshima, the founder of the Hōtokukai, the association for the edification of the modern nation), Tokyo: Kōshōkan Shoten.

Hankyurae, June 1, 2005.

Hasegawa, Koichi (2004), *Constructing Civil Society in Japan: Voices of Environmental Movements*, Melbourne: Trans Pacific Press.

Hasegawa Koichi (2005a), 'The development of the NGO activities in Japan: A new civic culture and the institutionalization of civic action,' in Robert Weller (ed.), *Civil Life, Globalization, and Political Change in Asia*, Oxford: Routledge/Curzon, 110–122.

Hasegawa, Koichi (2005b), 'Shimin shakai no koe: Kankyōshugi, riberarizumu and hosyusyugi' (Voices from civil society: Environmentalism, liberalism, and conservatism), *NIRA Seisaku Kenkyū*, 18(8): 13–18.

Hasegawa, Koichi (2010), 'Collaborative environmentalism in Japan,' in H. Vinken et al. (eds.), *Civic Engagement In Contemporary Japan: Established And Emerging Repertoires*, Berlin: Springer, 84–100.

Hasegawa, Koichi, Chika Shinohara, and Jeffrey P. Broadbent (2007), 'The effects of "social expectation" on the development of civil society in Japan,' *Journal of Civil Society*, 3(2): 179–203.

Hatamiya, Leslie T. (1993), *Righting a Wrong: Japanese Americans and the Passage of the Civil Rights Liberties Act of 1988*, Stanford: Stanford University Press.

Hechter, Michael (1987), *Principles of Group Solidarity*, Berkeley: University of California Press.

Hilo, Dilip (1992), *Black British, White British*, London: Paladin.

Home Office (2001), *Community Cohesion: A Report of the Independent Review Team*, London: Home Office.
Home Office (2004), *The End of Parallel Lives?: The Report of the Community Cohesion Panel*, London: Home Office.
Hong, Gyung-hee (2004), '21seiki, Chosen Soren no kaikaku to saisei no tame no tēgen' (21st century, a proposal for reform and revival of Chongryun), *Chongryun no saisei to dōhō shakai no hatten o negau fōramu 21*. Retrieved from http://www13.plala.or.jp/forum/teigen.html
Howard-Hassmann, Rhoda E. (2004), 'Getting to reparations: Japanese Americans and African Americans,' *Social Forces*, 83(2): 823–40. Retrieved from: http://www.humanities.manchester.ac.uk/socialchange/research/social-change/summer-workshops/documents/sleepwalking.pdf; http://www.urban.org/uploadedpdf/311373_nonprofit_sector.pdf; http://www.urban.org/uploadedpdf/311373_nonprofit_sector.pdf.
Huh, Dongchan (2003), 'Haewhae dongpowu ipjang: choil Pyungyang whaedamgwa ilbon chochongryun-"Miduhtun joguk" manhang shiinhoo Chochongryun sawhae Choonggyukae whipssayuh' (The stance of overseas compatriot: North Korea-Japan Pyongyang meeting and Chongryun-Chongryun community under a shock after the admission of the brutality by 'the belived homecountry'), *Bookhan*, 376: 93–99.
Institute of Community Cohesion (2008), *Understanding and Appreciating Muslim Diversity: Onwards Better Engagement and Participation*, Coventry: Institute of Community Cohesion.
Jin, Heekwan (1996), 'Bookhan gwha Chochongryun wue jungchi gyunggaejuhk sangwhansung' (Political and economic interrelations between North Korea and Chongryun), *Wallgan Tongil Gyungjae*, May.
Jin, Heekwan (2001), 'Chochongryun weu sunggyuk byunwha wa jaeil dongposawhae wue tonghap' (Change of Chongryun and the solidarity of *zainichi* compatriot society), *Overseas Korean Times*, 202: 14–21.
Kagoshima Jinjō Kōtō Shōgakkō (Kagoshima Higher Elementary School) (1922), *Kagoshima kōshi den* (Biographies of dutiful people of Kagoshima), publisher unknown.
Kagoshima Ken Aira Gun Kokubu Mura Kyōikukai (The Educational Committee of Kokubun Village, Aira Country, Kagoshima Prefecture) (1917), *Kōshi Kinzaemon* (Filial piety of Kinzaemon), Kagoshima: The Educational Committee of Kokubun Village, Aira Country, Kagoshima Prefecture.
Kagoshima Ken Ishin Shiryō Hensanjo (Kagoshima Prefectural Historiographical Institute of the Meiji Restoration) (ed.) (1971–1978), *Kagoshima ken shiryō kyūki zatsuroku kōhen and tsuiroku* (The collected historical materials of the Shimazu family and the Satsuma domain: Part II and supplementary volumes), Kagoshima: Kagoshima prefecture.
Kagoshima Ken Joshi Shihan Gakkō (Kagoshima Prefectural Female Teacher's School) (ed.) (1940), *Kyōdo fujin dokuhon* (Women of the home province), Tokyo: Kairyūdo.
Kagoshima Ken Kyōiku Chōsa Kai (Kagoshima Prefectural Educational Investigation) (1927), *Ōshima kaihatsu no onjin to kōshi sappu* (Patrons of

the development of Ōshima and dutiful men and women of Satsuma), publisher unknown.
Kagoshimaken Ken Kyōiku Iinkai (Kagoshima Prefectural Educational Investigation Committee) (1975), *Kagoshimaken no minka: kagoshimaken kinkyū minka chōsa hōkokusho* (The report on traditional private houses in Kagoshima), publisher unknown.
Kagoshima Kenritsu Sendai Kōtō Jogakkō Kōyūkai (The Graduates' Association of Kagoshima Prefectural Sendai Girls' High School) (1915), *Kōjoseppu den: Gotairei kinen* (Biographies of dutiful women: Commemorating the enthronement), publisher unknown.
Keizai sangyō shō (Ministry of Economy, Trade and Industry) (2010), *Tsūshō hakusho 2010 nen ban* (The 2010 white paper on international trade). Retrieved October 22, 2010, http://www.meti.go.jp/report/tsuhaku2010/2010honbun_p/index.html.
Kim, Hyuk-Rae and David McNeal (2005), 'From state-centric to negotiated governance: NGOs as political entrepreneurs in South Korea,' in Robert Weller (ed.) *Civil Life, Globalization, and Political Change in Asia*, Oxford: Routledge/Curzon, 95–108.
Kim, Mi-ryung (2000), '2000nen, dōhōno kitaini kotae shinrai kachitoritai: Zainichi Chosenjin jinken kyōkai- Huh, Kwang Su kaichōni kiku' (In 2000, we want to achieve the credit by responding to the expectation of the compatriots: From the president of *zainichi* Chosenjin Human right Association, Huh, Kwang Su), *Chosun Shinbo*, January 12. Retrieved from http://www1.korea-np.co.jp/sinboj/sinboj2000/sinboj2000- 1/sinboj20000107/sinboj20000112/sinboj2000011271.htm.
Kimura, Kunihiro (2000), 'Being unmarried under sex discrimination and inequality within the sexes: A simple model,' *Sociological Theory and Methods*, 15(2): 375–382.
Kimura, Kunihiro (2010), 'Sex-based discrimination trends in Japan, 1965–2005: The gender wage gap and the marriage bar,' in Miguel Angel Centeno and Katherine S. Newman (eds.), *Discrimination in an Unequal World*, New York: Oxford University Press, 156–171.
Kitayama, Glen Ikuo (1993), 'Japanese Americans and the movement for redress: A case study of grassroots activism in the Los Angeles Chapter of the National Coalition for Redress/Reparations,' M.A. Thesis, Los Angeles: University of California Los Angeles.
Koike, Shimpei, Mayuko Nakamaru, and Masahiro Tsujimoto (2010), 'Evolution of cooperation in rotating indivisible goods game,' *Journal of Theoretical Biology*, 264: 143–153.
Kono, Norio (2006), 'Shotoku bunpu to Gini Keisū ni kansuru ichi kōsatsu' (A note on the income distribution and the Gini Coefficient), *Keizai Kagaku Kenkyū* (Studies in economic science), 9(2): 51–69.
Ku, Dowan (2001), *Kankoku kankyō undō no syakaigaku* (Sociological analysis of the environmental movement in South Korea), Ishizaka Koichi and Minori Fukushima (translators), Tokyo: Hōseidaigaku Syuppankai.
Kundnani, Arum (2001), 'From Oldham to Bradford: The violence of the violated,' *IRR News*. Retrieved 15 July, 2007, http://www.irr.org.uk/2001/october/ak000003.html.

Lee, Changsoo and De Vos, George A. (eds.) (1981), *Koreans in Japan: Ethnic Conflict and Accommodation*, Berkeley: University of California Press.
Lee, Moon-woong (2004), 'Chongryungae jaeil Chosuninwue sengwhal chaegae: ilryuhakjuk jupguen' (The life system of Chongryun-affiliated *zainichi* Koreans: Anthropological approach), *Journal of Korean politics and society*, 26(1).
Lee, Wang-sae (1999a), 'Jaeil Chochongryun wue gwaguh, hyunjae, milae' (Past, present, and future of *zainichi* Chongryun), *Gyopo Jungcheck Jaryo* (Data for the policy for the overseas nationals), 59: 7–45.
Lee, Wang-sae (1999b), 'Chochongryun wue jojik gwa sanha danchae' (The system and affiliated groups of Chongryun), *Overseas Koreans Times*, 83: 16–22.
Lewis, Phillip (2007), *Young, British and Muslim*, London: Continuum International Publishing Group.
Li, Yanyan (in press), 'Growing strategies of non-profit organizations in Japan and China,' (forward) *The Asian Journal of Social Sciences*, 39(1).
Maki, Mitchell T., Harry H. L. Kitano, and S. Meagan Berthold (1999), *Achieving the Impossible Dream: How Japanese Americans Obtained Redress*, Chicago: University of Illinois Press.
Matsuo, Emiko (2008), Shōgunke okumuki no keizai: Goyō toritsugi minarai no kiroku kara' (The economy of Okumuki of the shogun family: Based on the record by an apprentice to goyo toritsugi),' *Tokyo to Edo Tokyo hakubutsukan kenkyū hōkoku* (Research report of the Edo-Tokyo Museum), 14: 47–61.
Matsuzaki, Rumi (2007), 'Chūkinsei ikōki ni okeru josei no yakuwari to okumuki: Satsuma han Shimazu ke wo jirei toshite' (Women's role and *oku* at the turning point between the middle ages and the Edo period: A case study of the Shimazu family in the Satsuma domain), *Hikaku kazoku shi kenkyū* (Journal of comparative family history), 21: 39–55.
Matsuzaki, Rumi (2008), 'Kinsei zenki kara chūki ni okeru Satsuma han Shimazu ke no josei to okumuki' (Women and *oku* in the case of the Shimazu family in the Satsuma-han from the beginning to the middle of the Edo period), *Rekishi* (Tohoku historical journal), 110: 19–46.
McCormack, Gavin and Haruki, Wade (2005), 'The strange record of 15 years of Japan-North Korea negotiations,' *Japan Focus*. Retrieved September 2, 2005, from http://japanfocus.org/_Gavan_McCormack_and_Wada_Haruki-The_Strange_Record_of_15_Years_of_Japan_North_Korea_Negotiations
McGhee, Derek (2008), *The End of Multiculturalism?: Terrorism, Integration and Human Rights*, Berkshire: Open University Press.
Mega, Atsuko (2008), *Kinsei no kazoku to josei: Zenji hōshō no kenkyū* (Family and women in early modern times: Research on commendations for good conduct), Osaka: Seibundō.
Michels, Robert (1911), *Paul Political Parties: A Sociological Study of the Oligarchical Tendencies of Modern Democracy*, Eden and Cedar (translators) (1915), New York: Hearst's International Library.
Millar, Jane (1996), 'Mothers, workers, wives: Comparing policy approaches to supporting lone mothers,' in Elizabeth Bortolaia Silva (ed.), *Good Enough Mothering?: Feminist Perspectives on Lone Motherhood*, London: Routledge, 97–113.

Ministry of Health, Labor and Welfare (Kōsei rōdō shō) (1983, 1988, 1993, 1998, 2003, 2006), *Zenkoku boshi setai tō chōsa* (National survey of single mother and other households), Tokyo: Ministry of Health, Labor and Welfare (Kōsei rōdō shō).

Morioka, Kiyomi (2002), *Kazoku shakai no 'ie' senryaku* (The '*ie*' strategy of noble families), Tokyo: Yoshikawa Kōbunkan.

Murray, Alice Yang (1995), *Silence No More: The Japanese American Redress Movement 1942–1992*, PhD. dissertation, Stanford: Stanford University.

Nagano, Hiroko (2003[1989]), 'Bakuhansei seiritsu ki no ie to josei chigyō' ('*Ie*' and female fiefs in the establishment period of the shogunate and domain system), republished in Hiroko Nagano (2003), *Nihon kinsei jendā ron: 'Ie' keieitai, mibun, kokka* (Gender theory in early modern Japan: '*Ie*' management entity, status and state), Tokyo: Yoshikawa Kōbunkan, 170–196.

Nagano, Hiroko (2003[1990]), 'Bakuhansei kokka no seiji kōzō to josei: Seiritsu ki wo chūshin ni' (Women and the political structure of Japan under the shogunate and domain system: The establishment phase), republished in Hiroko Nagano (2003), *Nihon kinsei jendā ron: 'Ie' keieitai, mibun, kokka* (Gender theory in early modern Japan : '*Ie*' management entity, status and state), Tokyo: Yoshikana kōbunkan, 197–235.

Nagano, Hiroko (2003), 'Meiji zenki ni okeru jendā no saikōchiku to katari: Edo no josei kenryokusha "Kasuga-no-tsubone" wo megutte' (The reconstruction of gender and narrative in the first half of the Meiji period: 'Kasuga-no-tsubone,' a powerful woman in the Edo period), in Mikito Ujiie, Yuki Sakurai, Masayuki Tanimoto, and Hiroko Nagano (eds.), *Nihon kindai kokka no seiritsu to jendā* (The founding of the modern state and gender in Japan), Tokyo: Kashiwa Shobō, 44–68.

Nagashima, Atsuko (2009), 'Sanae no uete wo meguru jendā (Gender in planter of sprouts of rice), *Rekishi hyōron* (Historical Review), 708: 31–45.

Nagel, Joane (1996), *American Indian Ethnic Renewal: Red Power and the Resurgence of Identity and Culture*, New York: Oxford University Press.

Naikaku fu kokumin seikatsu kyoku (Cabinet Office National Lifestyle Bureau) (2004), *Heisei 15-nendo kokumin seikatsu senkōdo chōsa* (The 2003 national survey of life preferences). Retrieved October 1, 2010 http://www5.cao.go.jp/seikatsu/senkoudo/h15/senkoudo15_1.pdf.

National Center for Charitable Statistics (2007), *The Nonprofit Sector in Brief: Fact and Figures from the Nonprofit Almanac 2007*. Retrieved November 30, 2010, http://www.urban.org/uploadedpdf/311373_nonprofit_sector.pdf.

National Federation of Single Parents and Children's Welfare Associations (Zenkoku boshi kafu fukushi dantai kyōgikai) (2010), *Yoikuhi wo kakuho suru tame no chōsa kenkyū jigyō hōkokusho* (Report: Research projects to obtain child support), Tokyo: Zenkoku boshi kafu fukushi dantai kyōgikai (National Federation of Single Parents and Children's Welfare Associations).

Neary, Ian (2002), *The State and Politics in Japan*, Oxford: Polity.

Nishimura, Tokitsune (1899), *Nantō ikō den* (Achievements of the Tanegashima family), Tokyo: Seishidō Shoten.

Noguchi, Takenori (1969), 'Okinawa Itoman fujin no keizai seikatsu: tokuni watakusā (shizai) ni tsuite (The economic life of women in Itoman, Okinawa:

About watakusā (private property) in particular),' *Seijo University Arts and Literature Quarterly*, 56: 11–35.

OECD (2007), *Babies and Bosses—Reconciling Work and Family Life: A Synthesis of Findings for OECD Countries*, Paris: OECD.

OECD (2010), Family database. Retrieved June 30, 2010, http://www.oecd.org/els/social/family/database

Oguma, Eiji (1996), *Tan'itsu minzoku shinwa no kigen: Nihonjin no jigazō no keihu* (The myth of the homogeneous nation: The history of the self-image of the Japanese), Tokyo: Shinyō-sha.

Okinawa Kaihatsu Chō Okinawa Sōgō Jimu Kyoku Sōmu Bu Chōsa Kikaku Ka (Okinawa Development Agency, Administration Bureau, Research & Planning Section) (ed.) (1974), *Okinawa no moai jittai chōsa* (A survey of rotating savings and credit associations in Okinawa), Okinawa Kaihatsu Chō Okinawa Sōgō Jimu Kyoku Sōmu Bu Chōsa Kikaku Ka.

Ono, Jūrō (1982), *Kyūshū no minka yūkei bunka no keifu (jō)* (Private houses in Kyūshū, a genealogy of tangible culture, 1), Tokyo: Keiyūsha.

Otabe, Yūji (2006), *Kazoku: Kindai Nihon kizokuno kyozō to jitsuzō* (Kazoku: Illusions and realities about the modern Japanese nobility), Tokyo: Chūō Kōron Shinsha.

Otabe, Yūji (2007), *Kazoku ke no josei tachi* (Women of noble families), Tokyo: Shōgakukan.

Phillips, Trevor (2005), 'After 7/7: Sleepwalking to segregation,' speech given at the Manchester Council for Community Relations, 22 September. Retrieved January 2, 2010 http://www.humanities.manchester.ac.uk/socialchange/research/social-change/summer-workshops/documents/sleepwalking.pdf

Policy Planning and Research Department, Ministry of Labor, Japan (1965–2005), *Chingin sensasu: Chingin kōzō kihon tōkei chōsa* (Basic Survey on Wage Structure).

Rampton, Anthony (1981), *West Indian Children in Our Schools*, London: Her Majesty's Stationery Office.

Rohlen, Thomas (1981), 'Education: Politics and prospects,' in Lee, C., and De Vos, G. (eds.), *Koreans in Japan: Ethnic Conflict and Accommodation*, Berkeley: University of California Press.

Runciman, Walter G. (1966), *Relative Deprivation and Social Justice: A Study of Attitudes to Social Inequality in Twentieth-Century England*, London: Routledge & Kegan Paul.

Ryang, Sonia (1997), *North Koreans in Japan: Language, Ideology, and Identity*, Boulder, CO: Westview Press.

Salamon, Lester M. (1992), *America's Nonprofit Sector*, New York: The Foundation Center.

Salamon, Lester M. (1995), *Partners in Public Service: Government-Nonprofit Relations in the Modern Welfare State*, Baltimore: Johns Hopkins University Press.

Santos, Fredericka Pickford (1975), 'The economics of marital status,' in Cynthia B. Lloyd (ed.), *Sex, Discrimination, and the Division of Labor*, New York: Columbia University Press, 244–268.

Sen, Amartya (1997[1973]), *On Economic Inequality*, expanded edition, Oxford: Clarendon Press.

Shihō Shō Chōsa Bu (Ministry of Justice, Research Division) (1942), 'Okinawa kenka ni okeru kyūkan moai ni tsuite' (The old custom of the rotating savings and credit association in Okinawa prefecture), *Setai chōsa shiryō* (Social research resources), 36: 163–189.

Shimazu, Nobuhisa (ed.) (2005), *Shimazu ke kyū Fukushōji bochi gaiyō (ryaku)* (An outline of the buried person and the location of their graves at the former Fukushōji temple (abridged)), Kagoshima: Shimazu Kenshōkai.

Shimazu, Tadashige (1983), *Rohen nangoku ki* (The memoirs of Tadashige Shimazu), Tokyo: The Shimazu Press.

Shimoebisu, Miyuki (2008), *Youikuhi seisaku ni miru kokka to kazoku: Boshi setai no shakaigaku* (Family, states, and child support policy: The sociology of single mothers), Tokyo: Keiso shobo.

Shoji, Yoko (1999), 'Kazoku seisaku (Family Policy),' in Shoji, Yoko, Kinoshita Yasuhito, Takegawa Shogo, and Fujimura Masayuki (eds.), *Fukushi shakai jiten* (Encyclopedia of the welfare society), Tokyo: Kobundo, 136–137.

Shōko Shūseikan (The museum of the Shimazu family) (ed.) (1985), *Shimazu shi seitō keizu* (The orthodox family tree of the Shimazu clan), Kagoshima: Shimazuke Shiryō Kankōkai.

Skinner, Christine, Jonathan Bradshaw, and Jacqueline Davidson (2007), *Child Support Policy: An International Perspective, Department for Work and Pensions Research Report 405*, Leeds: Corporate Document Services.

Statistical Bureau, Management and Coordination Agency, Japan (1965–2001, every year), *Rōdōryoku chōsa nenpō* (Annual Report on the Labor Force Survey).

Statistical Bureau, Management and Coordination Agency, Japan (1967, 1972, 1977, 1982, 1987, 1991, 1996), *Kokusei chōsa hōkoku, dai ichi-ji kihon shūkei kekka* (Population census of Japan, vol. 2, Results of the first basic complete tabulation).

Statistical Bureau, Ministry of Internal Affairs and Communications, Japan (2005–2006), *Rōdōryoku chōsa nenpō* (Annual Report on the Labor Force Survey).

Statistical Bureau, Ministry of Internal Affairs and Communications, Japan (2006), *Kokusei chōsa hōkoku: jinkō no danjo, nenrei, haigū kankei, setai no kōsei, jūkyo no jōtai* (Population census of Japan, vol. 2, Sex, age and marital status of population, structure and housing conditions households).

Statistical Bureau, Ministry of Public Management, Home Affairs, Posts and Telecommunications, Japan (2001), *Kokusei chōsa hōkoku: jinkō no danjo, nenrei, haigū kankei, setai no kōsei, jūkyo no jōtai* (Population census of Japan, vol. 2, Sex, age and marital status of population, structure and housing conditions households).

Statistical Bureau, Ministry of Public Management, Home Affairs, Posts and Telecommunications, Japan (2002–2004), *Rōdōryoku chōsa nenpō* (Annual Report on the Labor Force Survey).

Stockman, Norman, Norman Bonney, and Sheng Xuewen (1995), *Women's Work in East and West: The Dual Burden of Employment and Family Life*, London: UCL Press.

Sugano, Noriko (1999), *Edo jidai no kōkōmono 'Kōgi roku' no sekai* (Dutiful people in the Edo period, the world according to 'An official record of acts of dutiful devotion'), Tokyo: Yoshikawa Kōbunkan.

Sugano, Noriko (2001), '"Oi" wo toraeru onna to otoko no ishiki sa' (A gap in the awareness of 'aging' between women and men), in Yuki Sakurai, Noriko Sugano, and Hiroko Nagano (eds.), *Jendā de yomitoku Edo jidai* (The Edo period explained in terms of gender), Tokyo: Sanseidō, 238–273.

Sugano, Noriko (2008), 'Buke josei no shakai wo toraeru me: "Chiri zuka nikki no kentō kara' (Perspective of a woman of the samurai family on society: Analysis of *'Chiri zuka* Journal'), *Teikyō shigaku* (Teikyo journal of history), 23: 53–99.

Sugano, Noriko (ed.) (1999), *Kankoku kōgi roku* (An official record of acts of dutiful devotion), Tokyo: Tokyodō Shuppan.

Supreme Court General Secretariat (Saikō saibansho jimu sō kyoku) (2009), *Shihō tōkei nenpō 2008: kaji jikenn* (FY2008 Annual report of judicial statistics: Family cases), Tokyo: Hōsōkai.

Tai, Eika (2006), 'Korean activism and ethnicity in the changing ethnic landscape of urban Japan,' *Asian Studies Review*, 30: 41–58.

Takagi, Kazuyoshi (2010), 'Gendai America ni okeru syūkyō to seiji: New York ni okeru mosuku kensetsu wo megutte' (Region and politics in the current US: Thinking on the controversial New York mosque project,' Presentation at the Annual Meeting of Tōhoku Syakaigaku Kenkyūkai.

Takagi, Kazuyoshi (2010), 'Gendai America ni okeru syūkyō to seiji: New York ni okeru mosuku kensetsu wo megutte' (Region and politics in the current US: Thinking on the controversial New York mosque project), Presentation at the 2010 Annual Meeting of Tōhoku Syakaigaku Kenkyūkai.

Takahashi, Jere (1997), *Nisei Sansei: Shifting Japanese American Identities and Politics*, Philadelphia: Temple University Press.

Takahashi, Tetsuya (2007), 'Koreans under assault from the Japanese right,' *Japan Focus*. Retrieved March 12, 2007, from http://www.japanfocus.org/_Takahashi_Tetsuya-Koreans_Under_Assault_From_the_Japanese_Right.

Takayanagi, Mitsutoshi, Taishi Okayama, and Kazuma Saiki (eds.) (1964), *Shintei kansei chōshū shokafu daini* (The new Kansei edition of a compendium of genealogies of *daimyōs* and retainers No. 2), Tokyo: Zoku gunshoruijū Kanseikai.

Takezawa, Yasuko (1994), *Transformation of Japanese American Ethnicity: The Effects of Internment and Redress*, Tokyo: University of Tokyo Press.

Tanaka, Yayoi (2006), *NPO ga jiritsusuru hi* (When NPOs become independent), Tokyo: Nippon-Hyōron-sya.

Tanizaki, Jun'ichirō (1933), *Inei Raisan*, Thomas J. Harper and Edward G. Seidensticker (tranlsators) (1984), *In Praise of Shadows*, Tokyo: C.E. Tuttle.

Taylor, Charles (1991), *The Malaise of Modernity*, Cambridge: Harvard University Press.

The Shimazu Press (1978), *Shirayuki: Shimazu Tadashige Isoko tsuisō roku* (Reminiscences of Tadashige and Isoko Shimazu), Tokyo: The Shimazu Press.

Thoms, David and Tom Donnelly (2000), *The Coventry Motor Industry: Birth and Renaissance*, Hampshire: Ashgate Publishing Ltd.

Tokyo Daigaku Shiryō Hensanjo (Historiographical Institute of The University of Tokyo) (ed.) (1942–1966), *Dainihon komonjo iewake dai-16 Shimazu ke monjo no 1–3* (Historical documents of Japan by family: The Shimazu family documents 1–3), Tokyo: The University of Tokyo.

Torpey, John (2003), 'Politics and the past,' in John Torpey (ed.), *Politics and the Past: on Repairing Historical Injustices*, Rowman: Rowman & Littlefield Publishers, 1–34.

Trikha, Sara (2004), *2003 Home Office Citizenship Survey: People, Families, and Communities, Research Study 289*, London: Home Office.

Tsuchida, Kumiko (2008), 'Ethnic identities and sharing of the internment memories in the Japanese American Redress Movement,' in Koichi Hasegawa and Naoki Yoshihara (eds.), *Globalization, Minorities and Civil Society*, Melbourne: Trans Pacific Press, 58–71.

Tsujimoto, Masahiro (2000), 'Imin no keizaiteki tekiō senryaku to ippan kōkan ni yoru kyōryoku kōdō: Buenosuairesu ni okeru nikkeijin no keizaiteki kōsyudan' (The economic adaptation of migrants and the cooperative behavior by generalized exchange: The rotating credit association of Japanese migrants in Buenos Aires), *Japanese Journal of Social Psychology*, 16: 50–63.

Tsujimoto, Masahiro (2005), 'Shigen kōkan to kyōdōtai: Kōsyudan no syakai shinrigaku teki kenkyū' (Resource exchange and a community: Social psychological study on rotating savings and credit associations), *Annual Reports of the Graduate School of Arts and Letters Tohoku University*, 55: 64–76.

Tsujimoto, Masahiro (2006), 'Aruzenchin ni okeru nikkeijin no tanomoshikō: Ippan kōkan ni yoru keizaiteki tekiō senryaku' (Rotating credit associations of the Japanese in Argentina: Economic adaptation by generalized exchange), *Qualitative Research in Psychology*, 5: 165–179.

Tsujimoto, Masahiro (2008), 'Syakaiteki kōkan no seisei to iji: Okinawa no kōsyudan no tsuiseki chōsa' (A case study on social exchange: Rotating savings and credit associations in Okinawa prefecture), *Annual Reports of the Graduate School of Arts and Letters Tohoku University*, 58: 113–129.

Tsujimoto, Masahiro, Miyako Kuniyoshi, and Iwao Yokuda (2007), 'Okinawa no kōsyudan ni miru kōkan no seisei' (The genesis of resource exchange: A study of rotating savings and credit associations in the Okinawa Islands), *Japanese Journal of Social Psychology*, 23: 162–172.

Umemoto, Karen (1989), '"On strike!" San Francisco College Strike 1968–1969: The role of Asian American students,' *Amerasia Journal*, 15(1): 3–41.

Walthall, Anne (2001), 'Ōoku: Seiji to jendā no hikakushi teki kōsatsu' (A comparative-historical study on politics and gender about *Ōoku*), in Yuki Sakurai, Noriko Sugano, and Hiroko Nagano (eds.), *Jendā de yomitoku Edo jidai* (The Edo period explained in terms of gender), Tokyo: Sanseidō, 3–43.

Waters, Mary C. (1990), *Ethnic Options: Choosing Ethnic Identities in America*, Berkley: University of California Press.

Wei, William (1993), *The Asian American Movement*, Philadelphia: Temple University Press.

Yamagishi, Toshio and Mary C. Brinton (2010), *Risuku ni sewo mukeru Nihonjin* (Japanese who want to avoid risk), Tokyo: Kōdan-sha.

Yamamoto, Eric K. (1999), 'What's Next?: Japanese American Redress and African American Reparations,' *Amerasia Journal*, 25(2): 1–17.
Yamamoto, Eric K. (2001), *Race, Rights, and Reparations: Law of the Japanese American Internment*, New York: Aspen Law & Business.
Yamamoto, Hirofumi (2005), 'Bakufu ōoku to Satsuma han oku no kōsai ni tsuite: "Satsuma han oku jochū monjo" no kōsatsu' (The association between court ladies in the inner palace and Satsuma-han okujhochū documents in the collection of the historiographical institute), *Tokyo Daigaku Shiryō Hensan-jo kenkyū kiyō* (Research annual of the Historiographical Institute The University of Tokyo), 15: 113—132.
Yamaoka, Taku (2009), *Hoshigaranai wakamono tachi* (The young who want nothing), Tokyo: Nihon keizai shimbun-sha.
Yuval-Davis, Nira, Floya Anthias, and Eleonore Kofman (2005), 'Secure borders and safe haven and the gendered politics of belonging: Beyond social cohesion,' *Ethnic and Racial Studies*, 28(3): 513–35.
Zaidanhōjin Bunkazai Kenzōbutsu Hozon Gijutsu Kyōkai (The Japanese Association for the Conservation of Architectural Monuments) (1987), *Meishō Senganen tsuki Kekura kariya teien shūri kōji hōkokusho* (Report on the renovation of the garden in historical Kekura temporary residence), Kagoshima: Shimazu Limited.

Index

Act on the Promotion of Specified Non-Profit Activities (the 1998 NPO Act), 129
Akasaka, Norio, 114
Amino, Yoshihiko, 114
Anti-Vietnam War movement, 70, 74
Asian American movement, 70, 75–6, 78, 81, 140
Asō, Tarō, 117–18

Basic Plan for Gender Equality, 122
Beck, Ulrich, 85–6
Breadwinner, 26–8
Britishness, xii, 95–7
Brown, Gordon, 95–6

child support policy:
  current systems (Japan), 17–18
  France, x, 21–2, 25
  Germany, x, 21, 25
  history (Japan), 18–19
  Sweden, x, 20–1, 25–7, 29
  UK, x, 19, 23–5
  US, x, 19, 22–3, 25–7, 29–30
Chongryun, xi, 51–66, 139
Chosun Shinbo, 55, 59–60, 139
Civil Liberties Act of 1988, 69
Civil Rights movement, 59, 65, 70, 73, 80, 131
civil society, 62, 64–5, 113, 124–7
collective action, 58, 73, 100

commoner, x, xi, 32–4, 41–3, 47
community, 76, 79, 81
community cohesion, 83
concubine, 35, 40–1, 45–6, 48
countervailing power, 132

Democratic Party of Japan, 118
differentiation between religion and culture, 92–5
disturbances in Northern England, 83
Drucker, Peter, 128

early modern times, ix, x, xiii, Ch 3, 137–8
ethnic identity, x, 58, 81
ethnicity, ix, xii, 12, 62–5, 73, 75, 77, 80, 85, 89–90
expected value model of marriage, 2–4, 12

family policy, x, 26–9
feudal lord, x, 31, 33, 35–41, 46, 48
Free Speech movement, 70

Galbraith, J. K., 131
Gender Empowerment Measure (GEM), 122, 124
Gender-related Development Index (GDI), 124
gender roles, Ch 3, 31, 35, 46
gender system, 33, 45, 47–8, 50
gender wage gap, 2, 6–7
Giddens, Anthony, 85–6, 97–8

Index

government failure, 130, 133
Gramsci, 125
Great Hanshin Earthquake, 129
Griffin, Nick, 95–96
Ground Zero of the 9/11 terrorist attacks, 121

Habermas, 125
Harvard University, 119
hate crime, 121
Hatoyama, Yukio, 117–18
hereditary politician, xiii, 117–18
Human Development Index (HDI), 122, 124

identity management, xii, Ch 6, 85
IMD (International Institute for Management Development), 115–16
individualization, 86, 88–92
Inei raisan (In praise of shadows), 114
inequality within the sexes, 5, 9–10
Internal Revenue Service, 128
the Internet, 88, 97–8, 102, 119, 124, 141
the internment policy, 67–8, 71, 79
Inter-Parliamentary Union, 122
inward-looking youth, 113, 118
Iron Law of Oligarchy, 133

Japanese American Citizens League, 69
Japanese American redress movement, Ch 5, 67, 69, 140

legitimate wife, 35–7, 39–41, 45
Liberal Democratic Party (LDP), 19, 117–18, 129–30
life history, xi, 67, 69, 74, 80–1, 102, 108, 110, 112
Long-term Care Insurance, 61

market failure, 130, 133
marriage, ix, x, Ch 1, 1–8, 10, 12, 15, 32–3, 35–6, 38–9, 42–3, 47, 93–4, 96, 136
marriage bar, 3–4, 6–8
memory, 67, 69, 78
Michels, Robert, 133
Millar, Jane, 25
Mindan, Ch 5, 51, 53, 60–2, 64–5
modern times, 31–5, 43, 45–8, 50, 115
multiculturalism, 83–4
Muslims; see 'young Muslims'
mutual aid, 43, Ch 7, 100–2, 108, 112, 128

National Coalition for Redress/ Reparations (NCRR), 69, 72, 75–6, 78–82, 140
National Council for Japanese American Redress, 69
New Party Sakigake, 129–30
NGOs/NPOs, xiii, Ch 8, 124–8, 130, 132
North Korea, xi, 51–60, 62, 64–5, 139
not-for-profit, 125, 127
NPOs, xi, xiii, 63–5, Ch 8, 113, 124–35

Obama, President, 113–14, 120–1

obligation to maintain children, 15, 18, 28
Oguma, Eiji, 114
Okamoto, Tarō, 114
Okinawa, xii, xiii, 33, Ch 7, 100–3, 108–10, 118
oku, x, xi, 31–4, 36–9, 42–5, 47–9
omote, x, xi, 31, 34, 36–9, 41–5, 47–9

parallel lives, 83
Pearl Harbor attack, 67, 71, 73, 140
peer selection, 101–2, 107–8, 111, 141
Phillips, Trevor, 88
politicization, 71
post-bubble economic recession, 8, 119

reflexive modernity, Ch 6, 85–6, 97
reparation, xi, xii, Ch 5, 67–71, 76, 79–82, 139–40
resource mobilization theory, 131
ritual, 35–9, 41, 47, 138
rotating savings and credit associations (ROSCAs), xii, xiii, Ch 7, 100–12, 141

Salamon, Lester, 127, 132
samurai, 31–3, 35, 37, 41–3, 46–9
satori sedai (resigned, or impassive generation), 119
Satsuma, x, 33–41, 43, 45–7, 49, 137–8
Second World War, xi, 52, 67–71, 78, 87, 100, 108, 114, 140

Severe Acute Respiratory Syndrome (SARS) pandemic, 130
Shimazu family, x, xi, Ch 3, 33–41, 43–5, 47–9, 137–8
Social Democratic Party (SDP), 122, 129–30

Tanizaki, Jun'ichirō, 114
Tea Party Movement, 113, 121
Tokugawa shogunate, 31–6, 38–9, 40–1, 137
tokutei hi eiri katsudō hōjin (specified non-profit corporation), 124

United Nations Development Programme (UNDP), 122
unmarried women in Japan, x, 1–2

voluntary failure, 132

white supremacy, 72–3, 75
women's participation, xiii, 48, 113, 121–23
World Conference on Women in Beijing, 130
World Value Survey, 120
Yamaoka, Taku, 119

Yoshida, Shigeru, 117
young Muslims, xii, Ch 6, 83–9, 91–2, 94–5, 97–9, 141

zainichi, 51–2, 54–65, 139